# Birth of the Border

# BIRTH OF THE BORDER

## The Battle of Carham 1018 AD

Scotland and England and the Tweed
Betwixt

Rannoch Daly

Rannoch Daly is a former prison governor.
He lives in Coldstream with his wife, Evelyn.

Rannoch is a member of the Carham 1018 Society
(www.carham1018.org)
and the Bernician Studies Group of
Newcastle-upon-Tyne (www.bernicianstudies.eu).

**Birth of the Border; The Battle of Carham 1018 AD**

© Rannoch Daly 2018

Published by Wanney Books, NE66 1BT

Printed by Martins the Printers, TD15 1RS

ISBN: 978-1-9997905-5-4


Cover; The Tweed near Carham looking towards Birgham (Photo by Author)

Frontispiece; A tenth century stone cross from Carham in the ownership of the Society of Antiquaries of Newcastle upon Tyne. It is now in the Great North Museum: Hancock, Barras Bridge, Newcastle upon Tyne, NE2 4PT. It can be viewed on line at: http://www.ascorpus.ac.uk/catvol1.php?pageNum urls=60 (accessed 18 March 2018) Reproduced with Permission

This book is dedicated to the people of

# Bryneich

who have always lived

'both sides the Tweed'

## Names

The characters are British, Anglo-Saxon, Pictish, Scots, Welsh, Irish, Norse, Danish and Norman. Their name may first appear in the historical record in their own language or in another. Consequently, spellings vary: for example; Kenneth, Cyneth, Cinaed and Kyned are all the same person; as are Olaf, Olavr and Anlaf. Where more than one spelling is used I have used the variant which seems to me to correspond most closely to current conventional English: in these examples, Kenneth and Olaf. In direct quotes I have retained the spelling of the original author and, where it seems necessary for clarification, added my own preference in square brackets: for example; Cinaed [Kenneth II].

## Sources

Sources are indicated briefly in the text with name of author, date and page number in brackets: for example (Mack 1926: 6). Full details are in the bibliography.

## Abbreviations

ASC = Anglo-Saxon Chronicle (Whitelock 1961)
HE = Historia Ecclesiastica (Bede 1968)
HSC = Historia De Sancto Cuthberto (South 2002)
VSCA = Vita Sancti Cuthberti Anonymo (Colgrave 1939)
VSCB = Vita Sancti Cuthberti Beda (Colgrave 1939)

# Authors Preface

Soon after I came to live in Coldstream in 2007 I asked a member of the Local History Society about how the Tweed had become the border between Scotland and England. He told me about the Treaty of York, 1237. In 2014 I had a similar conversation with a member of the Battlefields Trust. He told me about the Battle of Carham, 1018: a discrepancy of 219 years.

After I joined the 'Carham 1018 Society', set up in 2014 to promote the 2018 commemoration of a thousand years since Carham, I was asked to write a booklet trying to explain why both answers were correct: 1018 as well as 1237.

In the process I learned about the Treaty of Falaise (1174) and the Quitclaim of Canterbury (1189) and much else. To tell the whole tale in such a short book requires the history to be somewhat condensed. However, this is my attempt.

# Acknowledgements

A book would have been impossible without the support and encouragement of Evelyn. I thank all the members of the Carham 1018 Society, particularly Peter Straker-Smith, Clive Hallam-Baker, David Constantine and especially David Welsh, who took on the Sisyphean task of trying to impart something of the historian's craft into my amateur efforts. The editing of Sue Ward made the book better than I had imagined was possible. The whole text was read by Jacquie Forrest, Catherine Hadshar and Neil McGuigan, whose suggestions led to many improvements. Despite their best efforts:

> The faults which remain are all mine, all mine.
> The faults which remain are all mine.*

*With apologies to Alan Hull and Lindisfarne


Rannoch Daly
Coldstream
2018

# Contents

# Introduction

 'A great battle was fought ....
at Carrum'

Rain is neutral: but as rain falls on the Pyrenees and runs north it becomes the water of French streams and rivers; and the rain which runs south becomes Spanish. The watershed of a mountain range is a natural geographical phenomenon, but it can also be adopted as a dividing line by people who wish to claim that their ethnicity, language, religion, etc is different from those on the other side: it can be used as a border between nations. In geographical terms, the opposite of a mountain range is a river valley but, as the Rhine demonstrates, rivers can also be used as borders.

The current borders within the British Isles vary greatly. Wales has both: it is much more mountainous than England and the two are divided, approximately, by the rivers Severn and Dee. Ireland is separated from Britain by the Irish Sea but, internally, the border between the Irish Republic and Northern Ireland has neither mountains nor rivers. Our focus here is on the border between Scotland and England: the Solway Firth, the Cheviot Hills and, especially, the river Tweed.

In 1926 James Logan Mack published his classic account of *The Border Line*. He had read everything on the subject he could get his hands on and he had walked every step from the Solway and Esk in the west, along the top of the Cheviots in the middle and down towards Berwick via the Tweed in the east. The border comes down from the Cheviot Hill and along the course of the Redden Burn as it flows into the River Tweed, close by the church of St Cuthbert in the village and parish of Carham.

> The Battle of Carham [---] in the year 1018 was the decisive factor in settling the easterly part of the Border Line, as the Scottish King, Malcolm II, claimed successfully, as a result of his victory, the whole country north of the Tweed. (Mack 1926: 6)

There are no eye-witness reports. The earliest surviving references to the Battle of Carham were written about one hundred years later by Simeon of Durham, who wrote in Latin and spells it 'Carrum'. Simeon's nineteenth-century translator, Joseph Stevenson, wrote in his Preface:

> Respecting the personal history of Simeon, monk and precentor of Durham, we have very little trustworthy information. The only fact connected with him upon which we can speak with confidence is that he was present at the entombment of the body of St. Cuthbert in the year 1104, at which time he was an inmate of that cathedral church. There is reason to believe that he died shortly after (AD 1129), at which period his chronicle terminates. (Simeon 1858: 5)

In his *History of the Kings of England* Simeon says:

> AD 1018. A great battle between the Scots and Angles was fought at Carrum between Huctred, son of Waldef, earl of the Northumbrians, and Malcolm, son of Cyneth, king of Scots, with whom there was in the battle Eugenius [Owain] the Bald, king of the Cumbrians (Simeon 1858: 113).[1] (see Box in Chapter 1: Cumbria and Strathclyde)

In his *History of the Church of Durham*, Simeon says:

> In the year of our Lord's incarnation ten hundred and eighteen, while Cnut ruled the kingdom of the Angles, a comet appeared for thirty nights to the people of Northumbria, a terrible presage of the calamity by which that province was about to be desolated. For, shortly afterwards, (that is, after thirty days) nearly the whole population, from the river Tees to the Tweed, and their borders, were cut off in a conflict in which they were engaged with a countless multitude of Scots at Carrum (Simeon 1865: 675). [2]

---

[1] Thomas Arnold gives Simeon's Latin original: 'Anno MXVIII. Ingens bellum apud Carrum gestum est inter Scottos et Anglos, inter Huctredum filium Waldef comitem Northymbrorum, et Malcolmum filium Cyneth regem Scottorum. Cum quo fuit in bello Eugenius Calvus rex Clutinensium.' (Simeon 1882: Vol 2, 155-6)

[2] Thomas Arnold gives Simeon's Latin original: 'Anno incarnationis Dominicae MXVIII, Cnut regnum Anglorum disponente, Northanhymbrorum populis per XXX. noctes cometa apparuit, quae terribili praesagio futuram provinciae cladem praemonstravit. Siquidem paulo post, id est, post triginta dies, universus a flumine Tesa usque Twedam populus, dum contra infinitam Scottorum multitudinem apud Carrum dimicaret, pene totus cum natu majoribus suis interiit.' (Simeon 1882: Vol 1, 84)

In his *History of Scotland* (1902) Professor Hume Brown gives Carham great significance. In his view, 1018 is to Scotland as 1066 is to England:

> [---] this final cession of Lothian is second in importance to no event in Scottish history. [---] Had Lothian remained in the possession of England the history of North Britain must have been so different that it is with Hastings rather than Bannockburn that Carham must be reckoned in the list of British battles. (Brown 1902: 43)

More recent assessments are provided by Professors Duncan, Barrow and Higham and by Tim Clarkson:

> It [Lothian] was recovered by the Scots in or just after 1018 when Malcolm II, hoping to take advantage of the uncertain position of Northumbria, launched an attack which met the levies of the land from Tees to Tweed under Earl Uhtred at Carham and thoroughly defeated them. [---] He [Uhtred] was then summoned to Cnut, who may have feared treason with Malcolm II, and was assassinated at court. His brother Eadulf was entrusted with the earldom, and gave Lothian to Malcolm II (who had doubtless recovered it) for a secure peace. (Duncan 1975: 97-8)

> By winning the battle of Carham on Tweed in 1018 Malcolm II made sure of permanent Scottish possession of Lothian [---]. (Barrow 1981: 25)

> Malcolm invaded Tweeddale and heavily defeated Earl Eadulf Cudel, Uhtred's brother[3], who was forced to cede the Lothians to Scotland as the price of peace. This decisive engagement led to the permanent loss of one of Bernicia's most prosperous provinces. (Higham 1993: 230)

> [---] to the Scots however, it was surely a military triumph which finally completed their hitherto piecemeal annexation of Lothian. [---] For Mael Coluim [Malcolm], then, the principal benefit of his victory at Carham was probably a substantial enlargement of his kingdom. (Clarkson 2014: 142)

The border was on the Tweed from 1018 but it was not on the Tweed *de jure* until the Treaty of York in 1237. Much water flowed in the Tweed between these dates. Among other events, there was the Scots occupation of Northumbria from

---

[3] Whether the men of Bamburgh were led by Uhtred or by his brother Eadulf is discussed in Chapter 5.

the 1130s to the 1150s, the Treaty of Falaise of 1174 and the Quitclaim of Canterbury in 1189.

This little book is like a sandwich. The battle is in the middle (Chap 5). The establishment of a border is a slow process. The book includes considerable background. Chapter 1 is a brief account of the early peoples who lived in or near Carham, who formed Bryneich (Bernicia) and then Northumbria. There was a long run-up to the Battle of Carham as the nascent Scotland and England engaged with the Vikings and Northumbrians (Chapter 2) and then with each other (Chapter 3). This leads up to the English crisis of 1016 (Chapter 4), the battle of Carham in 1018 (Chapter 5) and the immediate aftermath (Chapter 6). In the long follow-through after Carham Scotland and England had to engage with the Normans from 1066 (Chap 7) and then adjust to living with each other as neighbours (Chapter 8) before finding a border settlement in 1237 (Chapter 9).

An Appendix gives further information about Carham; the place, the church and the castle.

# 1

# Carham in Bryneich

 ## Bryneich before Northumberland

One outcome of the battle of Carham was that the ancient kingdom of Bryneich (Bernicia in Latin) was cut through the middle: the northerly part to Scotland (from the river Forth to the Tweed) and the southerly part to England (from the river Tweed to the Tyne). This chapter says a little about local prehistory; about the origins of Bernicia; its dominance of Northumbria in the 7th century, its key role in the early British church and the role of some of its kings as 'Bretwalda' of Anglo-Saxon Britain. 'The name Bernicia itself is anyway probably British. It appears in the form Bryneich in early Welsh poetry and that may well be its original form.' (Laycock 2008: 234) (Map 2)

The last Ice Age thawed sufficiently for north Britain to support human beings on a permanent basis about 12,000 years ago: the soils of Carham and the lower Tweed valley are mostly glacial deposits. Early peoples could walk to Britain across a land bridge from continental Europe (Doggerland) but, as the ice caps melted and the seas rose, the land bridge flooded. By about 6,500 BC 'Britain had become separated from the European landmass' (Passmore and Waddington 2009: Vol 2: 113, 140). Early Britons were hunter/gatherers of the Mesolithic Age (c.10,000 to 4,000 BC) and then farmers of the Neolithic Age (c. 4,000 to 2,500 BC).

The oldest residence in the vicinity is at Howick on the Northumberland coast where 'excavations revealed evidence for a circular, sunken-floored hut with post sockets and post pads for timbers that had supported a conical roof. The hut measured 6m in diameter and would have been sufficient for a family to live in. [---] The initial construction of the site has been radio-carbon dated to around 7,800 BC.' (Waddington and Passmore 2004: 25)

The Duddo Stone Circle and the cup-ring marked rocks on Chatton Park Hill provide further evidence of early human presence in the district around Carham. Henges, like the one at Milfield:

[---] can be found the length and breadth of Britain, from Orkney to Cornwall, and from Ireland to East Anglia. They are an insular British phenomenon, not having continental precursors like earlier enclosures and chambered cairns. The henge phenomenon provides the first evidence for a common cultural tradition that spans all of the British Isles, indicating a sense of cultural, and perhaps religious, unity. (Waddington & Passmore 2004: 66)

## Wark

Archaeological field-walking surveys near Wark, in the parish of Carham, have found numerous Mesolithic and Neolithic stone implements, in some instances more than 20 lithics per hectare (Passmore and Waddington 2009: Vol 1: 102-3). 'The regular clusters of Mesolithic material identified during this survey of the lower Tweed valley clearly identify this river as a major routeway for Mesolithic groups as well as an attractive area for settlement in its own right.' (Vol 2: 130-1).

## Sprouston

Ian M Smith (1991) has analysed in detail aerial photographs of crop marks at Sprouston, only three miles upstream from Carham. He reaches three conclusions:

- 'Phase I at Sprouston may thus embrace evidence of Mesolithic, Neolithic and Bronze Age activity; the earliest features being probably the interrupted ditched enclosure, perhaps the building beside the steading, the ring-ditch or barrow, together with those in the field to the south-east.' (269)

- In Phase II 'the fort and field-system coextensive with it are ultimately Romano-British.' (271)

- In Phase III 'we probably have the nucleus of a British estate adopted for use by the incoming English sometime in the late 6th or early 7th century, and successively elaborated for some 50 years or more thereafter.' (288)

# Carham – Romans – Votadini

The earliest written records of Britain are in Latin by Romans. Tacitus gives an account of a great speech by the Caledonian leader Calgacus before the Roman victory at the battle of Mons Graupius in 83 AD.[1]  However, by the following year, 84 AD, the Romans were hurriedly evacuating their Legionary fortress at Inchtuthil, north of Perth. Inchtuthil may have been a step too far.[2]

---

[1] According to Tacitus, Calgacus said: "You are united: you Caledonians have never been slaves. From here there is no retreat by land and even the sea offers no escape because of the Roman fleet [---] There are no more peoples behind us. There is nothing but rocks and waves - and the Romans are more menacing than them! [---]
They rob, kill and rape and this they call Roman rule. They make a desert and call it peace." (Salway 1981: 147)

[2] 'Striking evidence for the withdrawal was discovered at Inchtuthil. Buried in pits in the legionary workshops were found 3/4 ton (0.762 tonnes) of nails, all unused. They were presumably abandoned because it was not worth the effort of carrying them south, and buried so as to deny their use to the local tribesmen. The action of burial points to an ordered withdrawal.' (Breeze 2006: 102)

Map 1 - Carham in the Borders: Between Hadrian and Antonine

The earliest known map of Britain, produced by Ptolemy of Alexandria in about 150 AD, identifies a people called the Votadini in what is now south-east Scotland/ Northumberland and the Novantae in what is now Galloway. The Selgovae lived between these two (Jackson 1984: 4). Their language is likely to have been Britonnic, a predecessor of modern Welsh. Carham lay between the Votadini (perhaps the origin of the word 'Lothian') and the Selgovae (possibly the origin of the word 'Selkirk').

The Romans built Hadrian's Wall in the 130s AD and the Antonine Wall in the 140s AD. Carham sits halfway between the two walls with the substantial Roman fort of Trimontium only 20 miles west at Newstead, near Melrose. The Romans also established smaller temporary camps at Carham, Norham and East Learmouth (OS-Roman Britain: North Sheet). For three centuries of Roman occupation, Carham was in the middle of the border country (Map 1).

# The Coming of the Anglo-Saxons

The Romans left Britain in 410 AD to concentrate their efforts on other parts of their Empire. Around the year 540 AD, in *The Ruin of Britain*, the British monk Gildas wrote:

> As the Romans went back home, there eagerly emerged from the coracles that had carried them across the sea-valleys the foul hordes of 'Scottorum* Pictorumque', [---] They were to some extent different in their customs, but they were in perfect accord in their greed for bloodshed: and they were readier to cover their villainous faces with hair than their private parts and neighbouring regions with clothes. [---] So, they seized the whole of the extreme north of the island from its inhabitants, right up to the wall [Hadrian's wall]. (Gildas 1978: Chap.19.1)
>
> * 'The term "Scoti" was used from Roman times and into the early 8th century [---] to describe both Scots and Irish Gaels.' (Houston and Knox 2001: xvi)

# The Birth of Bernicia

Nennius was a later Briton who wrote around the year 800 AD. In his *Historia Brittonum* he tells of how the native Britons then invited the Angli and Saxones to come across the North Sea and help them against the Pictorum Scottorumque, including an account of how the Anglo-Saxons first settled 'in the north about the wall that is called Guaul [Hadrian's wall]' (see Box, Nennius: Historia Brittonum)

## Nennius: *Historia Brittonum*

'Chapter 31. Vortigern ruled in Britain, and during his rule in Britain he was under pressure, from fear of the Picts and Irish [Pictorum Scottorumque] and of a Roman invasion, and, not least from dread of Ambrosius*. Then came three keels, driven into exile from Germany. In them were the brothers Horsa and Hengest [---] Vortigern welcomed them, and handed over to them the island that in their language is called Thanet, in British Ruoihm.'

'Chapter 36. And it came to pass, after the English [the Anglo-Saxon newcomers] were encamped in the aforesaid island of Thanet, the aforesaid king promised to supply them with food and clothing without fail; and they agreed, and promised to fight bravely against his enemies.'

Vortigern married Hengest's daughter [Rowenna] and:

Chapter 38. Hengest said to Vortigern 'I am your father, and will be your adviser. Never ignore my advice, and you will never fear conquest by any man or people, for my people are strong. I will invite my son and his cousin to fight against the Irish ['Scottos'], for they are fine warriors. Give them lands in the north about the Wall that is called Guaul'. (Nennius 1980)

* Ambrosius was a fifth century Romanised Briton who opposed Vortigern's policy of engaging Saxon mercenaries (Salway 1981: Chapter 16).

In the years following the Roman withdrawal in 410 AD the land between the rivers Tyne and Forth became known as Bryneich (Bernicia in Latin). The capital was at a place called Din Guaire but Athelfrith, an Anglo-Saxon king of Bernicia, 'gave Din Guaire to his wife, whose name was Bebba, and it was named Bamburgh from his wife's name' (Nennius 1980: Chap 63). Other local place names of Anglo-Saxon origin include Carham, 'the place by the rocks', and its partner across the Tweed, Birgham, 'the place by the bridge (or crossing)'.

Photo 1: The rocks by the Tweed which give Carham its name with the church
and trees behind

## Lindisfarne, Catraeth, Degsastan

Towards the end of the sixth century the Anglo-Saxons of Bernicia won three
major battles against the native Britons: Lindisfarne, Catraeth and Degsastan.

At Lindisfarne, probably in the 580s:

> Four [British] kings fought against them [the Saxons]; Urien, and
> Rhydderch Hen, and Gwallawg and Morcant. Theodoric [the Saxon king]
> fought vigorously against Urien and his sons. During that time, sometimes
> the enemy, sometimes the Cymry [the Britons] were victorious, and Urien
> blockaded them for three days and three nights in the island of
> Lindisfarne. But during this campaign, Urien was assassinated on the
> instigation of Morcant, from jealousy, because his military skill and
> generalship surpassed that of all the other kings. (Nennius 1980: Chap
> 63)

Shortly before 600 AD an army of Britons rode south from Din Eidyn (Edinburgh) to fight the Saxons at Catraeth (modern Catterick). The dramatic poem *Y Gododdin*, written in Britonnic, describes the encounter. In contrast with King Malcolm's ride south to Carham in 1018, at Catraeth the Gododdin (the Votadini, the men of Lothian) were defeated. (see Box: Y Gododdin).

---

## Y Gododdin

Hero, shield held below his freckled brow,
His stride a young stallion's.
There was a battle-hill din, there was a fire,
There were swift spears, there was sunlight,
There was crows' food, a crow's tid-bit.
And before he was left at the ford,
As the dew fell, graceful eagle,
Beside the wave's spray, near the slope,
The world's poets pronounce him great of heart.
His war-plans cost him what by rights was his;
Wiped out, his picked warriors, by foe-men.
And before his burial below Eleirch Fre
There was valour in his breast,
His blood had washed over his war gear.
Undaunted, Buddfan ap Bleiddfan. (Clancy 1998: 53)

Note - "Y Gododdin" has two versions: 83 poems in the A text and 40 in the B text. This extract is a translation into modern English of the A text number 24.

---

At Degsastan, in 603 AD, Aedan mac Gabrain led the Scots of Dal Riata against the Saxons of Bernicia. We do not know the exact location of the battle of Degsastan (perhaps Dawston in Liddesdale) but we do know that the Bernicians won: 'thenceforward the Britons of Strathclyde remained the only serious rivals of the Angles of Bernicia for the possession of the Scottish Lowlands.' (Stenton 1971: 77) (see Box: Cumbria and Strathclyde).

## Cumbria and Strathclyde

Simeon describes Owain the Bald as 'rex Clutinensium'. The literal translation is 'king of the people of the Clyde' but it is sometimes translated as king of 'the men of the Clyde' or 'king of Strathclyde' or 'king of the Cumbrians'. Why the variety?

The Welsh word for Wales is 'Cymru'. The modern Welsh language derives from an ancient P-Celtic language, Britonnic. Prior to the coming of the Anglo-Saxons, Britonnic was the language of the native Britons. Cumbria, the present word for the Lake District, has the same root as Cymru: an ancient British word 'combrogi', meaning 'fellow-countrymen'.

The Anglo-Saxon invasion pushed the southerly Britons west towards what became Cymru (modern Wales). Similarly, as the Anglo-Saxons of Bernicia occupied Lothian and the Borders and spread west over the Pennines, the northerly Britons were also pushed west. They became concentrated in the valley of the river Clyde with a fortress at *Alt Clut* (the 'Rock of the Clyde', now known as Dumbarton Rock) and in the ancient British kingdom of Rheged, around the Solway. Rheged faded in the seventh century.

After the Norse sack of *Alt Clut* in 870 AD, the northerly Britons established a new base upriver at Govan/ Partick in the kingdom of *Strat Clut* (the 'Valley of the Clyde', Strathclyde). Their leaders were known as the 'kings of the Cumbrians', because that was what they called themselves, or the 'kings of Strathclyde', because that was where they lived. Their language is now known as Cumbric.

In due course, the name 'Cumbria' stuck with the southerly part, in modern England, whilst the name 'Strathclyde' referred to the northerly part, in modern Scotland. But this was a gradual process and in different centuries the words can have different meanings. Further ambiguity can arise: some historians refer to these people as 'Britons' and some prefer to call them 'Welsh'.

Note - A Cumbric remnant survives today in a Pennine sheep counting system; the basis of Harrison Birtwistle's 1984 opera "Yan, Tan, Tethera", which means "One, Two, Three".

The successes at Lindisfarne, Catraeth and Degsastan (Map 2) established Bernicia as a secure base for Anglo-Saxons in Britain but they also maintained:

> [---] extensive links between the Bernician dynasty and other Celtic kingdoms. For instance, when Aethelfrith was killed at the battle of the river Idle, his sons fled for refuge to Ireland and the Celtic kingdom of the Scots. Equally, between 653 and 657, Talorcan, son of a Pictish mother but the nephew of Oswiu of Bernicia, was a king of the Picts, and Oswiu himself may have married Rhiainnfellt, a princess of the British kingdom of Rheged. (Laycock 2008: 234-5)

Fig 1: Early Kings of Bernicia/ Northumbria

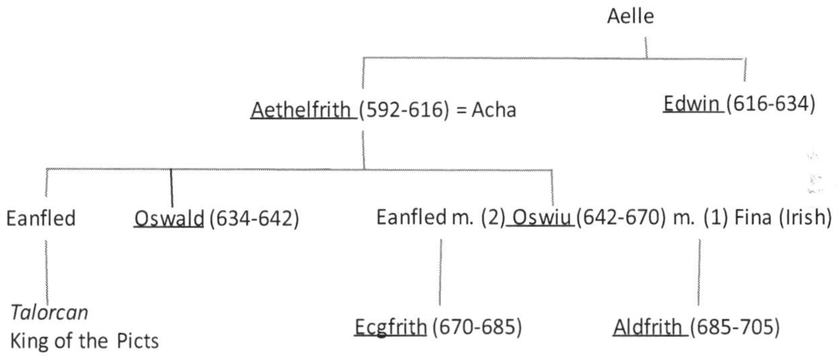

King Edwin of Deira was defeated by Aethelfrith of Bernicia, who became King of Northumbria in 604 AD. After exile in East Anglia, Edwin returned and defeated Aethelfrith in 616.

Aethelfrith's sons Oswald and Oswiu went into exile in Ireland but returned to defeat Edwin in 634.

After these two brothers the next two kings of Northumbria were Oswiu's sons Ecgfrith (by his second wife Eanfled) and Aldfrith )by his first wife Fina, an Irish princess).

Apart from Edwin, all these kings of Northumbria are sons or grandsons of the Bernician king Aethelfrith and his Deiran wife Acha, sister of Edwin.

It is significant that Edwin sought refuge in the Anglo-Saxon south-east but Oswald and Oswiu went to the Celtic north and west.

Their sister Eanfled married into the Pictish royal family and became mother of Talorcan, King of the Picts.

# Bernician Bretwaldas?

In early Anglo-Saxon Britain there were at least seven separate kingdoms of East Anglia, Essex, Kent, Mercia, Northumbria, Sussex and Wessex - the Heptarchy. At various times, a particular king would be recognised as 'Bretwalda', a sort of first among equals. In 604 AD the Bernician king Athelfrith conquered Deira (modern Yorkshire, approximately) to establish a single Kingdom of Northumbria from the Humber to the Forth. 'Northumbrian power extended westwards in 616 with the expulsion of the king of Elmet [modern West Yorkshire] and a victory at the battle of Chester [Map 2]. Later in the seventh century, Northumbria seems to have taken over the Kingdom of Rheged [Carlisle] and gained brief dominance over Mercia after Penda's death at the battle of the Winwaed in 655.' (Laycock 2008: 236) By the 670s Ecgfrith, king of Northumbria (670-685) was 'Bretwalda' or over-king of the Anglo-Saxons: that is, over most of southern and middle Britain.

However, in 685 AD, Ecgfrith overplayed his hand. He invaded Pictland but was defeated by Bridei, King of the Picts, at the battle of Dun Nechtain, near Forfar (Map 2).[3] Cadwallader Bates observes that: "In consequence of this signal disaster, the Picts recovered the territory occupied by the English to the North of the Forth, while the Scots of Dalriada and Britons of Strathclyde renounced the suzerainty of Northumberland." (Bates 1895: 66). Northumbria weathered this setback.

King Aldfrith (685-704), half-brother of Ecgfrith, ruled for the next twenty years, and died just before the Lindisfarne Gospels and the works of Bede were spreading the news across Europe that Northumbria was a powerful kingdom with a flourishing intellectual and cultural centre whose core was Bernicia.

Thus, the seventh-century people of Carham were living under the strongest power in Britain. It was no more than a long day's walk from Carham to the

---

[3] One of the miracles of prophecy attributed to Cuthbert when he was a bishop concerned the battle of Dun Nechtain. Cuthbert was accompanying Ecgfrith's queen Erminburg on a visit to Carlisle in 685 AD. They were looking at the city wall and the other Roman ruins: '[---] as Waga the reeve of the city, who was conducting them explained. The bishop [Cuthbert] meanwhile stood leaning on his supporting staff, with his head inclined towards the ground and then he lifted up his eyes heavenwards again with a sigh and said: "Oh! Oh! Oh! I think that the war is over and that judgment has been given against our people in the battle. [---] after a few days they learned that it had been announced far and wide that a wretched and mournful battle had taken place at the very day and hour in which it had been revealed to him. (VSCA: Chap 4.8)

centre of that power, Bamburgh. In the year 665 or thereabouts, Cuthbert, a monk but not yet a saint, walked that walk in the company of bishop Eata from the monastery of Old Melrose to the holy island of Lindisfarne.

Map 2 - Carham in Bryneich (Bernicia)

# The Church in Bernicia

After his defeat by Athelfrith in 604 AD, King Edwin of Deira went into exile in East Anglia at the court of King Raedwald; the likely subject of the Sutton Hoo ship burial (Carver 1998: 23). In the return match Raedwald assisted Edwin to defeat Aethelfrith in battle near the river Idle in 616 AD. Edwin's wife, Ethelberga of Kent, brought with her bishop Paulinus, an Italian sent by Pope Gregory to support Augustine of Canterbury's mission of 597 AD. Bede describes how

Paulinus "accompanied the king and queen to the royal residence at Ad-Gefrin [Yeavering] and remained there thirty-six days constantly occupied in instructing and baptising [---] in the nearby river Glen. This residence was abandoned by the later kings, who built another at a place called Maelmin [Milfield]. " (Bede 1968: Chap 2.14) Yeavering, Milfield and the river Glen are all within ten miles of Carham. Brian Hope-Taylor's archaeological study of Yeavering reported evidence which appeared to confirm Bede's account (Hope-Taylor 1977). (Map 2)

Athelfrith's sons Oswald and Oswiu were sent into exile in Ireland and Iona. When they returned and defeated Edwin in 634 AD they sent to Iona in 635 AD for Aidan to establish a monastery on Lindisfarne. Edwin acquired his Christianity from Rome via Canterbury, but Oswald and Oswiu acquired theirs from Ireland via Iona. On 5 August 641 Oswald was defeated and killed by Penda of Mercia at Maserfelth, which is possibly Oswestry in Shropshire. (Stenton 1971: 82)

## Synod of Whitby (664)

Conflict arose between the Ionan traditions of King Oswiu (642-671) and the Canterbury traditions of his wife Eanfled of Kent, particularly over the dating of Easter. Sometimes the royal household found themselves celebrating Easter twice: once for the king and once for the queen. Oswiu and his son Ecgfrith (r. 671-685) organised the Synod of Whitby in 664 to reconcile the two traditions (Map 2). Despite his own Ionan background, Oswiu opted for the Roman Easter, as we do today (Easter is the first Sunday after the first full moon after the spring equinox). Cuthbert had also been brought up in the Ionan tradition. He was not at the Synod (in 664 he was an obscure monk in Old Melrose) but he appears to have played a key role subsequently, with King Ecgfrith, in bringing the two traditions together.

# Northumbria in the Eighth Century

Northumbria had been the leading power in the seventh century, but the eighth century was not so glorious. Internally, the period was notable for feuding. Sometimes Bernicia was dominant and sometimes Deira: one king was deposed or killed by the next.

Northumbria controlled Lothian and the Tweed valley but not the lands of the Picts or the Scots or the men of Strathclyde. Northumbria had successfully defended itself against Mercia and the Welsh but never extended Northumbrian territory south of the Humber. They were not overrun, either from the north or the south, and despite the brief ascendancy of Mercia under Offa (died 796 AD) no other single power was strong enough to maintain dominance over all the others. Northumbria spent most of the eighth century as just one of the Anglo-Saxon Heptarchy. For further reading about Northumbria in this period I recommend Nick Higham (1993), David Rollason (2003) and Max Adams (2014).

# 2

# The Viking Effect

 ## Invasion and Occupation

In *Alfred's Britain* Max Adams gives a vivid account of the effect of the Viking raids and invasions of the ninth and tenth centuries (Adams 2017). One consequence was that the locals would band together to fight the Vikings instead of each other. The Anglo-Saxon kingdoms of the English Heptarchy began to meld. In the north there were moves towards unification by Picts and Scots.

In *A History of the Vikings* Gwyn Jones observes:

> The unexpectedness, the swiftness and the savagery of the Viking raid on the monastery at Lindisfarne in 793 came as a bolt from the blue not only to the monks surprised and slaughtered there but to Alcuin [of York] over in Charlemagne's court - 'it is some 350 years that we and our forefathers have inhabited this lovely land, and never before in Britain has such a terror appeared as this we have now suffered at the hands of the heathen.' (Jones 1984: 194)

## Danes

Viking raids continued throughout the early ninth century around the coast and particularly along the rivers. The limit of the tidal reach up-river from the sea was often close to a suitable ford: the point where the main sea routes met the main land routes and the old Roman road network. 'That network linked almost all the navigable heads of the major rivers: one giant communication and trading system.' (Adams 2017: 51, Map) In the early ninth century the Vikings had been using their raids around the British coast for plunder but also for reconnaissance. By 866 AD they knew the country well. Their invasion of that year was swift and effective.

Under their leaders Ivar, Halfdan and Hubba, ten thousand Danes spent the winter of 866-867 AD in the east of the country, including the sack of York in November 866. They killed Osbert of Bernicia (848-866) and his brother Aelle of

York (866-866) and in 867 they installed Ecgbert to run Northumbria. As Professor Duncan clarifies, Bernicia suffered under both the Danes and the Scots.

> The creation of the Danelaw after 866 left the ancient Northumbrian kingdom unable to resist an extensive Scandinavian settlement in Yorkshire, while north of the Tyne was terribly ravaged by Halfdan of York. But the Danes of Yorkshire seem to have desisted from harrying beyond Tyne after Halfdan's death in Ireland in 877, leaving a weak northern Anglian province, led, perhaps, by an ealdorman at Bamburgh, to face any enemy. From this situation, it seems, Giric [King of Scots] benefitted; the wars in which he subdued 'Bernicia' must have required army service in no small amount, for 'subduing' would be more sustained than the raids of Cinaed I [Kenneth MacAlpin] to Melrose and Dunbar. (Duncan 2002: 13)

## Hiberno-Norse

Whilst the Danes were on the east coast, other Vikings came to the west coast. By 840 they had progressed through Shetland, Orkney and the Hebrides to control the Irish Sea and to establish a major base for raiding and trading in Dublin; hence the term Hiberno-Norse. In 870 AD, after a four-month siege of Alt Clut ('Rock of the Clyde' = Dumbarton Rock):

> "[-—] the triumphant Vikings then stormed inside, looting and slaying and taking captives. Large numbers of Britons from the Rock and its hinterland were herded onto the waiting longships. Together with Picts, Scots and English captured in other raids, these unfortunates were taken to Dublin to be sold as slaves." (Clarkson 2014: 47)

Those Britons who survived regrouped further upstream at Govan/ Partick where they became known as the kingdom of *Strat Clut* (Strathclyde).

## Alfred the Great, King of Wessex

As the Danes spread out in the 870s overcoming one Anglo-Saxon kingdom after another it looked as if they might conquer the whole country. However, from a redoubt at Athelney, in the Somerset Levels, King Alfred of Wessex gathered support from the other Saxon kingdoms and began to push back. In 878 Alfred scored a notable victory over the Danes at Edington but this merely produced a stalemate. In an arrangement later formalised as the Treaty of Alfred and Guthrum (886) it was agreed that Alfred could rule south and west of a line

London/ Chester, but the Danes would rule east and north of this line. This area, later known as the Danelaw, roughly comprised 14 shires: York, Nottingham, Derby, Lincoln, Essex, Cambridge, Suffolk, Norfolk, Northampton, Huntingdon, Bedford Hertford, Middlesex and Buckingham (Lapidge 2008: 136). The most northerly is York.

With Alfred and Guthrum in a stalemate in the south, the church of St Cuthbert tried to effect a reconciliation in the north with the Danish, but Christian, king of Northumbria, Guthfrith. In 882 Eadred, an abbot from Carlisle, declared his support for the Danish regime in York. In return, Guthfrith granted land between Tyne and Tees to St Cuthbert's church, one of the roots of the Durham Palatinate. In 883 the community of St Cuthbert resettled at Chester-le-Street (Map 3). In 895 Guthfrith was buried in York Minster.[1]

The tussle between the Danes and the Anglo-Saxons varied across the country from all-out invasion to sporadic local wars and uneasy peace. One of the consequences was that the struggle against the Danes led the separate Saxon kingdoms into increasing cooperation. By the end of the ninth century England south of the Tees was beginning to look less like a heptarchy and more like a duopoly: English in the south and west (except Wales); Danish in the north and east (except Bernicia). Alfred of Wessex died in 899. Partly as a consequence of his efforts, the country he lived in became known as England rather than the Daneland it might have become.

Meanwhile in Scotland in the 840s Kenneth MacAlpin (843-858) became recognised as the first king of the Scots to also be accepted as king of the Picts: or, perhaps, according to Professor Dauvit Broun, the first king of the Picts to also be accepted as king of the Scots (Broun 2005). From MacAlpin onwards, the Picts and the Scots seem to have acted under one king rather than two.

---

[1] A tale of Guthfrith illustrates the alleged supernatural insight of St Cuthbert, about 200 years after his death.
'The head of the *familia* of St Cuthbert, Eadred of Carlisle, located Guthrith (apparently miraculously), who had been sold into slavery to an English widow, at Whittingham on the river Aln, halfway between the Tyne and the Tweed, redeemed him and presented him to the Danish army. Guthfrith had converted to Christianity while in captivity and this factor, together with the advocacy of the church of St Cuthbert, created the opportunity for establishing the first Anglo-Danish kingdom in which a single king was recognised by both the army of the Scaldingi and by the Northumbrians.' (Woolf 2007: 78)

Map 3 - Carham: Tenth Century

## Picts and Scots

The Picts left many fine stone monuments (Jackson 1984). They left no literature, but surviving place-names indicate that 'the Pictish language was P-Celtic and therefore akin to Welsh.' (Broun 2013: 83) One of the great mysteries of history is how the Picts and their language managed to disappear quite so swiftly and comprehensively in the 9th century. No evidence has been found of a mass genocide or a mass emigration. The threat from the Vikings, who raided the coast and the islands but never took the mainland, may have been sufficient to push the Picts and Scots into alliance and, eventually, integration.

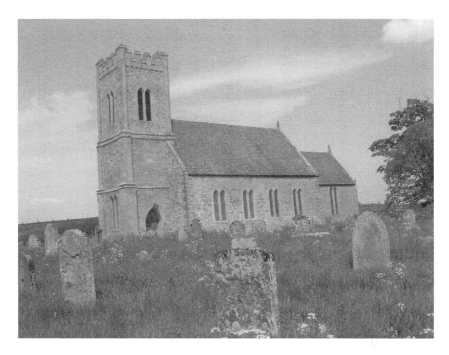

Photo 2: Carham; the Parish Church of St Cuthbert from the churchyard

# 3

# Northumbria: The Squeezed Middle

 ## The Confusing Tenth Century

By the year 900 AD the Danes were well established in northern and eastern England: the Hiberno-Norse were well established in Ireland and the western seaboard. The Anglo-Saxons south of the Humber were beginning to form one entity rather than several and the Picto-Scots were beginning to form a core group in the north to which others might gradually accrete. The corollary was that as the nascent English state started to edge its way north and the nascent Scottish state edged its way south they began to encounter each other directly. The Kingdom of Northumbria became the squeezed middle. The key dates are 920, 927, 945, 973 and 1006 AD.

## Alba

In the far north, Kenneth MacAlpin (843-858) had been succeeded by his brother Donald (858-862), then his two sons, Constantine (862-877) and Aed (877-878), and then by four of his grandsons: Eochaid jointly with Giric (878-889), Donald II (889-900) and then the long reign of Constantine II (900-943). At about this time, the name changed. Contemporary sources began to refer to Donald II and then Constantine II not as king of the Picts or as king of the Scots but as *ri Alban*, the king of Alba (Broun 2013: Chap 3). However, Alba did not yet include Orkney, Shetland, the Hebrides or the western isles, which were all Norse; or the Cumbrians in the kingdom of Strathclyde; or the Anglo-Saxons in Lothian, which was still part of Northumbria/ Bernicia; or Galloway, which was of mixed ethnicity and of no fixed allegiance.

## Hiberno-Norse

In 902 AD the Irish intervened. They expelled the Norse from Dublin and many of them arrived on the Irish Sea coasts of Galloway, Cumbria, north Wales and the Isle of Man. Undaunted, the Hiberno-Norse seem to have treated their enforced resettlement as both a challenge and an opportunity. The influence of the Norse language can still be traced in the place names in these parts suggesting that some of the Hiberno-Norse settled and stayed.

In 918 AD, at Corbridge on the Tyne (Map 3), a Northumbrian force led by Ragnald, a Norseman, defeated a combined force of Scots, under Constantine, and Bernicians, under Ealdred. The location of the battle, close to Hadrian's wall, indicates an attempted Scots invasion. Their defeat, however, left the Norse Ragnald in power in York as King of Northumbria. At about the same time his brother Sictric had prevailed in Ireland and was now back in charge in Dublin.

| Kings of England | | Kings of Scotland | |
|---|---|---|---|
| Edward | 899-924 | | |
| Athelstan | 924-939 | 900-943 | Constantine II |
| Edmund | 939-946 | | |
| Eadred | 946-955 | 943-954 | Malcolm I |

# First Exchange 920 AD

King Edward of Wessex, following his father Alfred's policy of consolidation, was now the undisputed Anglo-Saxon leader south of the Humber. In 920 he took this further in what appears to be a non-aggression pact with:

> the king of the Scottas and all the people of the Scottas and Ragnald, and the sons of Eadwulf [Bernicians], and all who live in Northumbria, both English and Danish and Northmen and others, and also the king of the Strathclyde Welsh and all the Strathclyde Welsh (Whitelock 1961: ASC Text A). (see Box: The Anglo-Saxon Chronicle)

Woolf describes this as 'the earliest recorded diplomatic exchange between a kingdom that can be legitimately regarded as ancestral to Scotland and one that can be legitimately regarded as ancestral to England.' (Woolf 2007: 146)

# Athelstan at Eamont 927 AD

Ragnald died in 920. He was succeeded at York by his brother Sictric. After King Edward's death in 924 his son Athelstan became king of England. Sictric died in

# The Anglo-Saxon Chronicle

During the reign of Alfred the Great (871-899), scribes in Winchester collected together all the annals, histories and records of the past that they could muster and collated them in chronological order in Old English. Some of the content about early years is legendary and mythical but, as the records reach the years 800 and 900, they become more factual. The Chronicle was copied and taken to other centres. These were copied in turn and continued with varying degrees of detail into the 10th, 11th and 12th centuries.

Several versions have come down to us from Winchester (Text A and G), Abingdon (Text B and C and the *Annals of St Neots*), Worcester (Text D), Peterborough (Text E) and Canterbury (Text F). We do not know through how many transcriptions each may have travelled from the original. From our point of view, there are two particular problems:

1.As the place names above show, the Chronicles were mainly written in the south. Their compilers may have had limited, and perhaps garbled, information about events north of the Humber. Even the so-called 'Northern Recension' of Peterborough is actually a twelfth century copy of a Kentish version after the Peterborough original was destroyed by fire in 1116 (Swanton 1996: xxi-xxviii).

2.The Chronicles are written from the Anglo-Saxon viewpoint (not the viewpoint of the Britons or Danes or Scots or Norse, etc) so may contain an element of bias, conscious or unconscious, rather than even-handed history.

Consequently, historians of the medieval period must put some effort into comparing the various Chronicle texts with each other and setting them beside other sources and deciding which is the most likely. Several modern editions have been prepared and published, for example Whitelock (1961) and Swanton (1996).

927 and Athelstan took York for himself and then proceeded north for another diplomatic agreement with:

> Hywel, king of the west Welsh, and Constantin, king of the Scottas and Owain king of the people of Gwent*, and Ealdred, son of Eadwulf, from Bamburgh. And they established peace with pledges and oaths in the place which is called Eamont [Map 3], on 12 July, and renounced all idolatry, and afterwards departed in peace. (Whitelock 1961: ASC Text D)

> * In this context 'Gwent' probably means Cumbria/Strathclyde (Woolf 2007: 151)

William of Malmesbury claims that at Eamont 'the English king received Constantin's son from the font'. Given that the feast of St Hildulf is on 11 July this child may have been the future King Ildulf (954-962): all part of the diplomacy. (see Woolf 2007: 193)

The parties to the Peace of Eamont 'renounced all idolatry', which looks like a pact against the Viking pagans. Ragnald of York had been a party to the agreement of 920 but he was not at Eamont in 927 and neither were any other Vikings.

In his *History of the Kings* Simeon reports that in 934 AD Athelstan ravaged the east of Scotland:

> A. D. 934. Ethelstan, the valiant king of the Angles, - because Constantine, king of the Scots, had broken the league which he had made with him, - set out for Scotland with a strong naval force and no small army of cavalry. But in the first place, going to the tomb of St Cuthbert, and honouring him with a royal donation of lands and other property, he ravaged Scotland with his land force as far as Dunfoeder [Dunottar: Map 3] and Wertermore [Fortriu], and with his navy as far as Caithness, and in a great measure depopulated it. In consequence, king Constantine was compelled to give him his son as a hostage, with suitable offerings; and the peace being renewed, the king returned to Wessex. (Simeon 1858: 88)

In addition, 'Constantine *sub-regulus*' (under-king) is listed as the first witness to a charter of Athelstan issued at Buckingham on 12 September 934. He is also listed as principal guest (Owain of Strathclyde is listed second) at a 'great plenary court at Cirencester' in 935 (Woolf 2007: 167). However, Constantine was then at least 60 years of age and there were younger contenders for the throne in

Scotland. Perhaps looking after his interests back home, Constantine next appeared in England in 937 fighting against Athelstan at the battle of Brunanburh.

## Brunanburh

In October 937 a combined force of Norse (under Olaf), Scots (under Constantine) and Cumbrians (leader unnamed) fought Athelstan at Brunanburh. Although it is clear that this was in the north, the locale is not known for certain (some writers favour The Wirral: Map 3). All accounts agree that despite huge losses on both sides, all the leaders survived. Although Athelstan seems to have prevailed, his victory was short-lived; he died at Gloucester on 27 October 939 and was succeeded by his brother Edmund. However, the Northumbrians rejected Edmund and 'were false to their pledges and chose Anlaf[Olaf] as their king'" (Whitelock 1961: ASC Text D)

Olaf, a Hiberno-Norse, formed an alliance with his cousin, Olaf Sictricsson of the Five Boroughs (Leicester, Nottingham, Derby, Stamford, Lincoln). In 941 the first Olaf led an army north to harry Bernicia, but he died on campaign at Tyninghame, East Lothian. Olaf Sictricsson took over but lost the Five Boroughs to King Edmund and was replaced in 943 by Ragnald Guthfrithson.

# Edmund cedes 'Cumbraland' 945 AD

In 945 Edmund of England drove the Norse leaders out of Northumbria and then invaded Strathclyde.

> The contemporary Anglo-Saxon Chronicle states that Edmund ravaged all 'Cumbraland' [Strathclyde], and gave it to Malcolm, king of Scots, on condition that he should be Edmund's fellow-worker by sea and land. According to Roger of Wendover 'two sons of Dunmail, king of Strathclyde, were blinded by Edmund's orders' (Stenton 1971: 359)

Perhaps Edmund and Malcolm preferred each other as allies rather than enemies, particularly against the Hiberno-Norse. In the tenth century much of the political relationships between kingdoms was based on the personal relationships between kings and, on a personal level, the alliance was shortlived; Edmund died on 26 May 946 to be succeeded by Eadred. Edmund had endeared himself to his people by dying 'in a most honourable way: while going to the help of one of his officers who was being attacked by a felon with a dagger.' (Humble 1980: 107)

In this period, the succession of rulers at York was rapid and fractious:

937 - Athelstan, as King of England (dies 939)
939 - Edmund, as King of England
939 - Olaf Guthfrithson of Dublin: after York rejected Edmund
942 - Blacaire Guthfrithson after his brother Olaf dies
945 - Edmund, King of England: on seizing York
946 - Ealdred, as King of England, after his brother Edmund is stabbed
948 - Eric 'Bloodaxe': after York rejected Ealdred
948 - Ealdred, as King of England: after ousting Eric 'Bloodaxe'
949 - Olaf Sictricsson; a Dublin Norse
952 - Eric 'Bloodaxe' reinstated
954 - Oswulf of Bamburgh appointed Earl of Northumbria by Ealdred, King of
England, after Eric 'Bloodaxe' killed on Stainmore by 'Maccus', of Bamburgh.

## Scots gain Edinburgh 954-962 AD

Whilst the Northumbrians were pre-occupied with their frequent changes of
ruler, during the reign of the Scots king Ildulf (954-962), '[-—] Edinburgh was
abandoned to the Scots. A Northumbrian earl who must grasp York firmly and
obey a royal master in Winchester or Bath had little time for a rock fortress lying
as far to the north as London is to the south.' (Duncan 1975: 95)

| Kings of England | | Kings of Scotland | |
|---|---|---|---|
| Eadred | 946-955 | 943-954 | Malcolm I |
| Edwy | 955-959 | 954-962 | Ildulf |
| Edgar | 957-975 | 962-966 | Dubh |
| | | 966-971 | Culen |
| Edward | 975-978 | 971-995 | Kenneth II |

# Edgar Cedes Lothian 973 AD

Edgar became king of England on 1 October 959 after the death of his brother
Edwy, aged about nineteen. Edgar seems to have been particularly attracted to
ceremony and to the church. He and Dunstan, Archbishop of Canterbury,
planned a second coronation service in 973, a record of which survives showing

that some elements were still in use at the coronation of Queen Elizabeth II in 1953. Edgar's ceremony took place at Bath on Whit Sunday 973, just after he had passed the age of thirty, the age below which one could not become a priest. Stenton (1971: 369) reports the sequel:

> Three manuscripts of the Chronicle state that after Edgar had been crowned he sailed with his fleet to Chester [Map 3], where six kings came to him and promised to serve him by sea and land. [-—] Florence of Worcester asserts that Kenneth, king of Scots, Malcolm, king of the Cumbrians, Maccus, king of many islands, and five other princes named Dufnal, Siferth, Huwal, Jacob and Juchil swore fealty to Edgar at Chester, and afterwards rowed him on the Dee from his palace to the church of St John and back again, while he held the rudder.

At about this time, according to the *De Primo Saxonum Adventu (Of the First Arrival of the Saxons*, an early twelfth century Durham document, possibly also by Simeon) Earls Oslac and Eadwulf, along with bishop Aelfsige:

> conducted Cinaed [Kenneth II] to king Edgar. And when he had done homage to him, king Edgar gave him Lothian; and with great honour sent him back to his own. (Woolf 2007: 211)

There are potential problems in interpreting what happened between Kenneth and Edgar on this occasion and in similar encounters from the tenth to the early thirteenth centuries. If any of these encounters resulted in a joint communiqué, few have survived. As is the case today, diplomatic 'solutions' can be rather short documents which don't go into every detail. Each side can then apply their own 'spin' to convince their supporters that they are the winners. For many of these encounters between the Scots and the English the only remaining accounts are from English sources and we don't know to what extent they may have been 'spun' in the English favour. Woolf wryly observes that: 'This event, which if it happened can be dated to the period 968-75, was subsequently used to justify claims that Scottish kings held Lothian of the English crown, and the account may have been fabricated for this purpose.' (Woolf 2007: 211)

## Ethelred the 'Unready'

King Edgar of England died on 8 July 975. He had two sons: Edward, from his first marriage, aged around fifteen, and Ethelred, from his second marriage, who was about ten. Edward took the throne but on 18 March 978 he was murdered outside Corfe castle in Dorset. Ethelred and his mother Aelfryth were both at the castle at the time and thereby implicated in the death of Edward, who later became known as Edward 'the Martyr'. Ethelred later became known as 'the Unready'. Ethelred means 'wise counsel' and Unred means 'unwise counsel' or 'evil trickster' but the later soubriquet 'Unready' rather obscures this biting pun. King Ethelred was consecrated king at Kingston-upon-Thames shortly thereafter. He was still only about thirteen years old and the events at Corfe left the impression of a child king in the hands of an unscrupulous mother. Perhaps surprisingly, Ethelred was to be king of England until 1016; on the throne for 38 years, the longest of all the Saxon kings.

## Annals and Chronicles

The Anglo-Saxon Chronicle provides useful information about England and the Anglo-Saxon view of the world in the 10th century. The Annals of Ulster provide a similar Irish record but there is no Scottish equivalent. The Chronicles of the Kings of Alba (CKA) provides a sketchy king list but for the years 980 to 1018 AD it is very sketchy indeed. Thus, for the crucial years leading up to the battle of Carham, we have few local Scottish sources. In the table of kings below, the "?" beside Giric and Kenneth III indicates uncertainty (see Duncan 1975: 628).

| Kings of England | | Kings of Scotland | |
|---|---|---|---|
| Edward | 975-978 | 971-995 | Kenneth II |
| Ethelred | 978-1016 | 995-997 | Constantine II |
| | | ?997-1005 | ?Giric |
| | | ?997-1005 | ?Kenneth III |
| Cnut | 1016-1035 | 1005-1034 | Malcolm II |

# Malcolm's Siege of Durham 1006 AD

From about 990 to about 1010 the English were continuously harassed by the Danes. Ethelred's only strategy seemed to be to pay them off with Danegeld which, of course, merely encouraged them to keep coming. We know from English sources that in 995 AD Kenneth II, king of the Scots, invaded Northumbria. The church community of St Cuthbert fled from Chester-le-Street to Ripon and then to Durham (Map 3). Kenneth was beaten off by Uhtred, son of the Earl of Bamburgh. In 1005 AD King Kenneth III was killed at Monzievaird by Malcolm II, who succeeded him. Malcolm decided that he too would invade Northumbria. After being bested by Uhtred at Durham in 1006 he limped back to Scotland to lick his wounds. King Ethelred rewarded Uhtred by making him Earl of York as well as Bamburgh, reuniting Northumbria under one ruler. For the moment, Uhtred was in the ascendant. (see Box: Simeon's Account of the Siege of Durham: 1006 AD).

## Simeon's Account of the Siege of Durham: 1006 AD

[-—] during the reign of Ethelred, king of the English, Malcolm, king of the Scots, the son of king Kyned [Kenneth II], collected together the entire military force of Scotland; and having devastated the province of the Northumbrians with the sword and fire, he laid siege to Durham. At this time bishop Aldun had the government there; for Waltheof, who was the earl of the Northumbrians, had shut himself up in Bebbanburc [Bamborough]. He was exceedingly aged and in consequence could not undertake any active measures against the enemy.

Now, when this young man [Uhtred] perceived that the land was devastated by the enemy, and that Durham was in a state of blockade and siege, he collected together into one body a considerable number of the men of Northumbria and Yorkshire, and cut to pieces nearly the entire multitude of the Scots; the king himself, and a few others, escaping with difficulty. He caused to be carried to Durham the best-looking heads of the slain, ornamented (as the fashion of the time was) with braided locks, and after they had been washed by four women, - to each of whom he gave a cow for their trouble, - he caused these heads to be fixed upon stakes, and placed round about the walls.

When king Ethelred heard of this, he summoned this young man [Uhtred] to his presence (this was during the lifetime of his father Waltheof) and as a reward for his courage, and for the battle which he had fought so gallantly, he gave him the earldom which had been his father's, adding thereto the earldom of the men of York. (Simeon 1865: 765)

The broad picture was as follows. In 945 King Edmund had ceded 'Cumbraland' to the Scots, in c. 960 Edinburgh had been abandoned to the Scots and in 973 King Edgar had ceded 'Lothian' to the Scots. Each of these developments suggest a recognition of the status quo in the tenth century: the growth of Scots presence and Scots influence and Scots power south of the Forth. The failure of the Siege of Durham in 1006 was a setback but the southward momentum would be restored in 1018 by the battle of Carham.

# 4

# The English Crisis of 1016

 ## Cnut the Conqueror

The crisis had two roots: the effectiveness of renewed Danish invasions and the ineffectiveness of Ethelred's defence. The origins of the crisis lay in the 980s.

Alex Woolf quotes the Annals of Ulster: 'AU 986.3 Iona, of Colum Cille, was plundered by the Danair on Christmas Night, and they killed the abbot and fifteen of the elders of the monastery.' (Woolf 2007: 217) He explains:

> The most likely candidate as leader of these Danes is Olafr Tryggvason who would briefly go on to be king of Norway c. 995-1000. He was first named, as the leader of a fleet of ninety-three vessels at Folkestone, in the Anglo-Saxon Chronicle for 991, but his fleet is almost certainly that which attacked Watchet in north Devon in 988. (p 218)

Tryggvason continued across the Thames estuary in 991 to engage with the English in Essex at the Battle of Maldon. The victory was to the Vikings: Ethelred paid Danegeld of £22,000 in gold and silver to Olaf. (See Box: Battle of Maldon - 991)

## Svein, King of England 1013

It is perhaps an indication of the character of Svein Forkbeard that in 987 he 'was involved in the killing of his own father' and in 999 'he was involved in the killing of his old comrade in arms Olafr Tryggvason.' (Woolf 2007: 223) Svein followed Tryggvason's example with repeated attacks on England. Stenton mentions raids on coastal Wessex in 997; Dorset, Hampshire and Sussex in 998; Kent in 999; west Sussex, south Devon and Somerset in 1001; £24,000 of tribute money in 1002; Wessex in 1003; East Anglia in 1004; Sandwich, the south east, Hampshire, Berkshire, the Chilterns and Wiltshire plus £36,000 in tribute money in 1005 (Stenton 1971: 379-381).

## The Battle of Maldon - 991

'The Battle of Maldon' is a poem of several hundred lines in Old English which describes a heroic but disastrous defeat at the hands of the Danes. Below are lines 1106-1112 of the original and a translation by Wilfrid Berridge, in which he has followed the Anglo-Saxon poetic preference for alliteration over rhyme.

If anyone had written a contemporary poem about the battle of Carham this is what it would have looked like.

### The Battle Is Joined

Þær wearð hream ahafen, hremmas wundon,
earn æses georn; wæs on eorþan cyrm
Hi leton þa of folman feolhearde speru,
gegrundene garas fleogan;
bogan wæron bysige, bord ord onfeng.
Biter wæs se beaduræs, beornas feollon
on gehwæðere hand, hyssas lagon.

Now was riot raised, the ravens wheeled,
The eagle, eager for carrion, there was a cry on earth.
Then loosed they from their hands the file-hard lance,
The sharp-ground spears to fly.
Bows were busied - buckler met point
Bitter was the battle-rush, warriors fell
On either hand, the young men lay!

Note
Text from these websites (both accessed 14 March 2018)
Original
http://english.nsms.ox.ac.uk/oecoursepack/maldon/index.html
Translation - http://www.battleofmaldon.org.uk/poem-2.html

After a few years respite, Svein returned to East Anglia, eastern Mercia and then west to Wiltshire in 1009. 'A chronicler writing in the following year estimated that, apart from East Anglia, they had ravaged the whole or part of fifteen counties in the sixteen months since they came to land in 1009.' (Stenton 1971: 383) In 1011 they raided Kent. By 1013 England was near to collapse under the repeated raids and tribute payments which only served to encourage the Danes further. Svein realised that more than booty might be available. He was already King of Denmark; perhaps he could be King of England as well.

Svein landed at Sandwich and proceeded up the east coast, up the Humber and up the Trent to Gainsborough (Map 3). In the north he was immediately welcomed by Northumbria, Lindsey and the Five Boroughs. After Uhtred submitted to him, Svein proceeded south and west into Mercia where Oxford surrendered but London did not. He marched west to take Wessex and then returned across central England back to Gainsborough, where he died on 3 February 1014. 'By this time, according to the Chronicle, *"the whole nation regarded him as king in all respects."'* (Stenton 1971: 385) He was king; but he was never crowned.

# Cnut, King of England 1016

Svein's son Cnut returned briefly to Denmark after his father's death but was back in England in 1015, clearly intent on the throne. The populace was split: some favoured Cnut; some rallied round Ethelred, who returned from exile in Normandy but who died on 23 April 1016 (Roach 2017: 308). His son, Edmund 'Ironside', continued the struggle. Uhtred supported Edmund's campaign in Chester but, whilst Uhtred was in the west, Cnut pushed north towards York. Uhtred hurried back, recognised Cnut's military superiority and surrendered to him. Cnut appointed Eric Hlatthir as Earl at York and then fought it out with Edmund across southern England.

In October 1016, on an island in the River Severn near Deerhurst, they agreed a partition. Edmund took Wessex and Cnut took all the rest but, when Edmund Ironside died on 30 November 1016, Cnut claimed the whole country. Edmund's two infant sons Edmund and Edward were evacuated to safety in Sweden (Edward 'the Exile' returned forty years later - see Chapter 7). Cnut was crowned at Westminster on Christmas day 1016. In the summer of 1017 he consolidated his position by marrying Emma of Normandy, widow of Ethelred. Later in 1017 he felt sufficiently confident to disband his fleet and:

> in a national assembly held at Oxford, his leading followers and Englishmen from all parts of the country came to an agreement about the terms on which they could live together. It was decided that the system of legal relationships which had prevailed in Edgar's reign should form the basis of the new Anglo-Danish state, and an oath to observe "Edgar's law" was taken by all members of the assembly. It is with the

> departure of the Danish fleet and the meeting at Oxford which followed
> it [in 1018] that Cnut's effective reign begins. (Stenton 1971: 399)

On Christmas Day, 1016, after over 150 years of Anglo-Danish war, Cnut was the first Dane to be crowned king of the English. The Saxon dynasty of Ethelred the Unready and Edmund Ironside had collapsed. Malcolm II was king of Scots and in alliance with Owain of Strathclyde. In Bamburgh Castle, Uhtred was piggy in the middle.

# 5

# The Battle of Carham 1018

 ## Malcolm and Owain and Uhtred

This chapter looks at the battle itself. It also considers three matters of historical controversy; the first two already well under way and a third which may arise shortly:

- Was the battle in 1016 or 1018?

- Was the leader of the men of Bamburgh Uhtred, as stated below, or his brother Eadwulf 'Cudel'?

- Were the relics of St Cuthbert in nearby Norham at the time and thus a potential motivating factor for the participants in the battle?

By 1018 Malcolm II (1005-1034) had been king of Scots for thirteen years. He had not forgotten his defeat at Durham in 1006.

Owain the Bald seems to have become king of Strathclyde in 1015. He was at Carham in support of King Malcolm II but Owain also had his own incentive: to assert his authority over southern Cumbria; modern Carlisle.

Uhtred was earl of Bamburgh but with his nose out of joint. In the battle for the English throne he had backed the loser, Edmund, against the winner, Cnut. He was then humbled when Cnut installed Erik of Norway as earl at York. Uhtred knew he was not a favourite south of the Tees.

## The Military

What was the nature of military force in 1018? A few of the more powerful kings could afford to keep some troops with axes, knives, spears, swords, shields and horses and even to import mercenary soldiers from elsewhere, but not in vast numbers. A small band of trained men could form a mounted raiding party seeking plunder but an army intending to invade and conquer would be likely to need large numbers of marching men: boots on the ground. There were no guns or explosives. Archery was used for hunting animals and for sniping at individuals but massed ranks of bowmen, such as at Crecy (1346) were a development of later centuries. Horses were mainly for transport and for specialist roles such as scouting. Many soldiers could not afford a horse: they were infantry who had to fight hand to hand, face to face.

## The Site

As Map 4 shows, Carham lies on the south bank of the Tweed about halfway between Cornhill and Sprouston with the village of Birgham opposite on the north bank. About two miles to the east of Carham is the site of the castle of Wark and immediately to the east of Wark is a pair of crossed swords indicating the site of the battle of Carham (1016). We will examine the question of the date in some detail below. The site is also controversial and does not appear on recent editions of Ordnance Survey maps.

Simeon's description of the battle taking place 'at Carrum' probably refers to the parish of Carham in general rather than to the hamlet of Carham in particular. In any case, battles rarely take place at a precise spot. A pair of crossed swords on a map indicates the general vicinity but it may have ranged over a wide area. Lines of troops can spread out over a considerable distance. If they charge, they may not all charge at once. There are flanking movements and feints and chases, and the battle usually has a beginning, a middle and an end; often not on the same spot.

An extensive study of the geomorphology of the Till-Tweed basin has identified the area east of Wark as one where the Tweed has changed course over the centuries (Passmore and Waddington 2009: Fig. 2.51). It is quite likely that a thousand years ago this area was either under water or at least so marshy that it would have been an impossible site for a battle. Having considered the lie of the land, the Carham 1018 Society have concluded that a more likely site is west of Wark nearer to Carham church and Carham Hall.

## The Route

A medieval army marching out of the Scottish Highlands would most likely cross the River Forth a few miles upstream of Stirling at the Fords of Frew. The route south then keeps to the east of the River Clyde and, if they are heading for Northumbria, needs a suitable spot to ford the River Tweed. Malcolm and Owain probably met up in the Peebles area, perhaps at Caddon Lea (Woolf 2007: 238-9). They could have crossed the River Tweed between Birgham and Carham, but they probably did not: an army is rarely more vulnerable than when trying to emerge from a water crossing. If they were expecting to meet Uhtred's men anywhere near Carham, it would have made sense to cross the Tweed further upstream and then proceed down the south bank. The Tweed and the Teviot meet at Kelso. A crossing upstream from Kelso would have involved crossing two smaller rivers rather than the united waters downstream.

## The Location

It would probably have suited the Scots to get beyond Carham and across the river Till into more open country but if Uhtred could hold the Scots at Carham that would have suited the men of Bamburgh. The Scots would have been vulnerable at the Birgham/ Carham ford or they would have been squeezed between the northern slopes of the Cheviot Hills and the southern banks of the Rivers Tweed and Teviot. It is a potential bottleneck. The fact that they met at Carham suggests that Uhtred had intelligence of their approach and raised his forces in time to meet them at a desirable spot.

Birgham/ Carham appears to have been a long-established key point for fording the Tweed. It was in Bamburgh's strategic interest to retain control of the crossing. In addition, in 1018 Carham was still part of the patrimony of St Cuthbert. The bishopric was now based in Durham but the spiritual root was Lindisfarne, adjacent to Uhtred's base at Bamburgh. The men of Bamburgh were fighting to preserve their territory, of which Carham had been an integral part both strategically and spiritually for several centuries. (see Appendix: Carham - the place)

## Between Redden and Duddo

In geographical terms, Carham is an unusual place. It is the only place in England which has Scotland on three sides. Standing in the Carham parish churchyard, Scotland is to the north, the west and the south. Like an English salient, Carham protrudes westwards from the Duddo Burn at Cornhill-on-Tweed. The border between Scotland and England might easily have headed uphill towards the Cheviot from Carham's eastern parish boundary on the Duddo Burn rather than from the western boundary on the Redden Burn, as it does now. Carham might now be part of Scotland rather than part of England. Perhaps the battle of Carham set the border not only on the Tweed but also on the Redden rather than the Duddo. (Map 4)

Map 4 - Battle of Carham: Site and Date?

This old Ordnance Survey map shows the date of the battle as 1016 and the site of the battle east of Wark castle. As Chapter 5 clarifies, the date has now been determined as 1018 and the site is more likely to have been west of Wark castle, near Carham Hall.

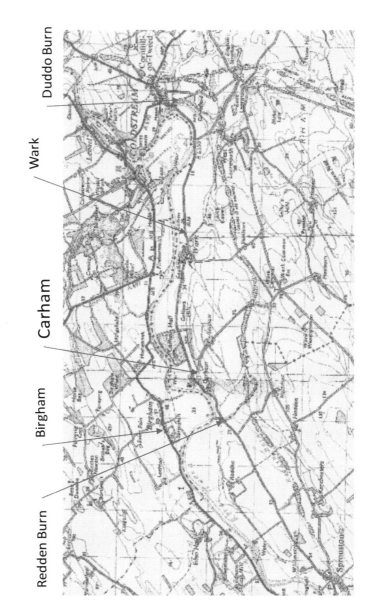

Redden Burn        Birgham        Carham        Wark        Duddo Burn

## The Outcome

We have no details of the numbers of casualties on either side but from Simeon's summary, it sounds devastating:

> nearly the whole population, from the river Tees to the Tweed, and their borders, were cut off in a conflict in which they were engaged with a countless multitude of Scots at Carrun. When the bishop [Aldun] heard of the miserable destruction of the people of St Cuthbert, he was smitten to the heart with deep grief [-—] a few days afterwards he was seized with sickness and died. (Simeon 1865: 675)

## The Silence of the Angles

English sources such as the Anglo-Saxon Chronicle do not mention the battle of Carham. Since the English played no part in the battle, this is understandable. The Scots did not push south of the Tees: Eric Hlatthir of York was untouched and Cnut, king of England, was untroubled. According to Simeon, the losers were 'nearly the whole population, from the river Tees to the Tweed'. Cnut was content, for the moment, to let it go.

# Controversy: 1016 or 1018?

In the above account the battle took place in 1018 and the leader of the men of Bamburgh was Uhtred. Some historians have taken a different view. This section includes relevant extracts from the *Anglo-Saxon Chronicle*, from Simeon and from modern historians and presents this writer's conclusions.

According to the *Chronicle* entry for 1016:

> "[-—] the Atheling Edmund [Ironside] rode to Northumbria to Earl Uhtred, and everyone thought that they would collect an army against King Cnut. Then they led an army into Staffordshire and into Shropshire and to Chester, and they ravaged on their side and Cnut on his side. He then went out through Buckinghamshire into Bedfordshire, from there to Huntingdonshire, and so into Northamptonshire, along the fen to Stamford, and then into Lincolnshire; then from there to Nottinghamshire and so into Northumbria towards York. When Uhtred learned this, he left his ravaging and hastened northwards, and submitted then out of necessity, and with him all the Northumbrians and he gave hostages; *and nevertheless he was killed and with him Thurketel, Nafena's son; and then*

> *after that the king (\*E: Cnut) appointed Eric for the Northumbrians, as*
> *their earl, just as Uhtred had been*; and then turned him (\*E: they turned
> them) southward by another route keeping to the west and the whole
> army then reached the ships before Easter." (Whitelock 1961: ASC 94-95,
> quoted by Duncan 1976: 20-28, italics and punctuation by Duncan)

(\*E: indicates a variation in Chronicle Text E)

In *A History of the Kings of England* Simeon's account of these events in 1016 follows the Chronicle account above so closely that he almost certainly had a copy to hand (Simeon 1858: 108). In addition, in his *Account of the Siege of Durham (De Obsessione Dunelmi)* Simeon[1] says:

> But upon the death of Ethelred [23 April 1016], when Cnut became
> possessed of the whole realm of England, he sent a message to the earl
> [Uhtred], commanding that he would come to him as his lord. Having
> received a safe conduct for his journey there and home again, the earl
> went. Upon the day appointed, as he was going to the king to treat of
> peace, certain of the king's armed soldiers, who were hidden within the
> traverse of the house at Wiheal, behind a curtain which was there
> suspended, suddenly rushed out and killed the earl, and forty of the
> chiefest of his men, who had entered along with him. This was planned
> by the treachery of a certain powerful man, Turebrant [also known as
> Thurbrand], surnamed Hold. (Simeon 1865: 766-7)

Thus, Simeon had a detailed account of the death of Uhtred and he had a Chronicle to hand which appeared to tell him that this took place in 1016. However, Simeon's own entry for 1018 states that Uhtred was at the Battle of Carham in 1018 (Simeon 1858: 113 quoted in the Introduction to this book).

In his magisterial *Anglo-Saxon England* (1943) Sir Frank Stenton takes the *Anglo-Saxon Chronicle* at face value. He says that Uhtred was killed in 1016 and, 'as names are better remembered than dates', the battle of Carham must also have taken place in 1016 or earlier (Stenton 1971: 418). Stenton mentions the Carham comet (Simeon 1865: 675, quoted in the Introduction to this book) but he does not consider its potential for dating the battle.

---

[1] Modern scholarship suggests that *De Obsessione Dunelmi*, which is a short document of only four pages, may not have been written by Simeon.

## Simeon's Eclipses

Peter Hunter Blair notes twelve datable items, including five eclipses in the years 733, 734, 752, 756 and 796 on which Simeon's dates and times of the day correspond precisely with the eclipse canon of J. Fr. Schroeter, the most accurate mapping of historical European eclipses up to that date (Schroeter 1923: 85). Blair concludes 'Of these twelve items the entries relating to the five eclipses are the most valuable for the evidence they provide of chronological accuracy.' (Blair 1963: 96)

## Simeon's Comet

In an article in the Scottish Historical Review (SHR) in 1976 Professor Duncan shows that Simeon's description of the Carham comet matches a comet of 1018 documented in 1889 by George F. Chambers, the leading writer on astronomy of the period (Duncan 1976: 20-28). Tim Clarkson demonstrates in even greater detail that Simeon's dating of the comet 'is supported by contemporary records from China, Korea, Japan, Germany, Italy and Ireland.' He reports an entry for 1018 in the Annals of Ulster: 'A comet appeared this year for the space of a fortnight in the autumn season.' After referring to Gary Kronk, the noted twenty-first century astronomer and author of Cometography Vols 1-6, especially Vol 1 (Kronk 1999: 168-170), Clarkson continues: 'Detailed collation of contemporary observations and descriptions indicates that the phenomenon was first seen on 3 August 1018, when it was noticed by Chinese observers. It remained visible in the skies over China for thirty-seven days before passing out of view on 8 September.' (Clarkson: 2014: 136) It would be remarkable if this was not Simeon's comet.

## Anglo-Saxon Chronicle (ASC)

If the astronomical record indicates that the battle was in 1018, why does the Anglo-Saxon Chronicle appear to say that Uhtred was killed in 1016? In the same SHR article of 1976 mentioned above, Professor Duncan subjects the Chronicle entry for 1016 to rigorous cross-examination. His detailed textual analysis, his precise correlations with other datable events and his comparisons with other contemporary annals suggest two relevant conclusions. Firstly, that the annal for the year 1016 was written up subsequently, but 'no later than the end of 1019'. Secondly, that the phrase *'and nevertheless he was killed.....',* italicised in the extract above, was later information from 1018 (or possibly 1019) added to the entry for 1016 because both dealt with Uhtred. (Duncan 1976: 20-28)

The astronomical record and Duncan's textual analysis both look convincing. The battle of Carham took place in 1018, probably in September.

# Controversy: Uhtred or Eadwulf?

Simeon records that Uhtred was succeeded by his brother Eadwulf Cudel. If Uhtred had been killed in 1016 then he could not have been at the battle of Carham in 1018 so it would be logical to draw the conclusion that at the Battle of Carham the leader of the men of Bamburgh was Eadwulf. Some historians say Uhtred and some say Eadwulf. Two who give their reasons are Duncan and Clarkson.

## The case for Uhtred?

Duncan (1976) argues that it made no sense for Cnut to dispose of Uhtred in 1016. The population of York was very Viking and if they were to fight for Cnut they would do so more willingly under Eric of Norway. Uhtred, with his previous record of victory over Malcolm II in 1006, would be effective at Bamburgh in guarding the northern flank. It was only when Uhtred failed, by losing the battle of Carham in 1018, that it became evident to Cnut that Uhtred was of no further use so, at Cnut's behest, Thurbrand killed Uhtred soon thereafter.[2] In Duncan's view, in 1018 the battle of Carham was lost by Uhtred. Uhtred's brother Eadwulf took over at Bamburgh in late 1018 or early 1019.

## The case for Eadwulf?

On the other hand, Clarkson (2014) argues that it would have been unreasonable to expect Cnut to trust Uhtred and leave him in power in Bamburgh in 1016. The more sensible course would have been to kill Uhtred in 1016, appointing Eric in his place as Earl at York, and leaving Eadwulf to look after Bamburgh. In Clarkson's view, in 1018 the battle of Carham was lost by Eadwulf, who remained in charge at Bamburgh.

---

[2] Later, Thurbrand was killed by Ealdred, earl of Northumbria, son of Uhtred;
later again, Ealdred was killed by Carl, son of Thurbrand;
later still, several of Carl's sons were killed by Waltheof, son of Earl Siward, whose mother was the daughter of Ealdred.
This was not just a family feud; it was a great northern power struggle. Richard Fletcher (2002) examines this in considerable detail.

## Does it matter?

When Malcolm and Owain attacked in 1018 neither Eric, earl of York, nor Cnut, king of England, came to the aid of Bamburgh. Perhaps the Scots' ravaging was sufficiently focused on the land north of the Tees that neither Eric nor Cnut felt threatened. Whether the leader of the Bamburgh forces at the battle of Carham was Uhtred or Eadwulf is an intriguing puzzle, but it is of little consequence either way. This author names Uhtred throughout but accepts that it might have been Eadwulf.

# Controversy: St Cuthbert's Relics?

Recent unpublished research has raised the possibility that at the time of the Battle of Carham in 1018 the relics of St Cuthbert may have been in Norham, only ten miles downstream from Carham (McGuigan 2015). This possibility has prompted my speculation that this might have been a factor in the motivation of the participants in the Battle of Carham.

After Cuthbert's death in 687 his relics were interred on Lindisfarne. The *Historia de Sancto Cuthberto* records that Bishop Ecgred (830-845):

> transported a certain church, originally built by St Aidan in the time of King Oswald [634-642], from the isle of Lindisfarne to Norham and there rebuilt it, and translated to that place the body of St Cuthbert and [that] of King Ceolwulf [-—] (South 2002: Chap 9).

Simeon's *A History of the Church of Durham* tells us that Cuthbert's relics 'for seven years wandered up and down the whole province' (Chapter XXVII) accompanied by bishop Eardulf (Chapter XX) before settling in Durham in the charge of bishop Aldun in 995 after one hundred and twelve years at Cunacacestre (Chester-le-Street) (Chapter XXXVI). This is the widely accepted view (Gallyon 1977: 56).

However, McGuigan's careful review of early sources suggests that the relics may have been at Norham for about one hundred and eighty years rather than the thirty years indicated by Simeon. For example, according to the twelfth century historian William of Malmesbury (c.1095-c.1143), in his *Gesta Pontificum Anglorum* [Deeds of the Bishops of England], there was an attempt to move St Cuthbert's relics to Ireland but instead:

The body was taken to *Ubbanford... iuxta amnem Twda* [Norham], where it lay until the time of King Aethelred (reigned 978-1016). (McGuigan Section 3.3.1)

In addition, the early 11th century saints' burial list known as the *Secgan* 'took its final form sometime after 1013, when Florence was interred in Peterborough, but before 1031, by which time it had to have been entered in the Stowe manuscript.' The *Secgan* says:

Then lies St Cuthbert in the place known as Ubbanford, near the water that is known as the Tweed. (McGuigan Section 3.3.3)

McGuigan concludes: '[-—] the *Secgan*, suggests that it [the body of Cuthbert] lay at Norham-on-Tweed until 1013x1031. [-—] moving from Norham to Durham sometime in the early eleventh century.'

McGuigan does not suggest that these findings could have any implications for the battle of Carham in 1018. However, Norham-on-Tweed is only ten miles downstream from Carham. Could Cuthbert's relics have been resident at Norham in 1018? Could Norham have been a target of Malcolm's attack? Could Norham have been a target of Uhtred's defence? If Cuthbert's relics were in Norham in 1018, why does Simeon say they were in Durham? Simeon was a monk of the church of St Cuthbert at Durham: he lived beside Cuthbert's remains. He spent much of his time writing the history of Cuthbert's church. Did he not know? Did he know and not say? Or is Simeon's account the one which is accurate?

For this author, the possibilities raised about St Cuthbert's relics are more significant than the question of whether the Earl of Bamburgh at the time was Uhtred or his brother Eadwulf. However, this is speculation based on unpublished findings and I should not push speculation too far: I merely raise the possibility.

Fig 2: Malcolm and Uhtred and their descendants

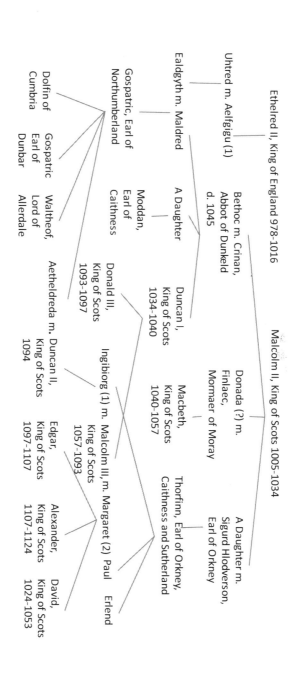

The interlocking pattern of marriage alliances and descent between the houses of England, Scotland, Northumbria and Orkney. Ingibiorg, the first wife of Malcolm III, may have been either the widow or the daughter of Thorfinn, Earl of Orkney. Dolfin of Cumbria was deposed from Bamburgh by the Normans but appointed Earl of Dunbar by the Scots king Malcolm III.

Sources: A H Dunbar 1906: Scottish Kings, A Revised Chronology of Scottish History 1005-1625, 2nd Edition, Edinburgh, David Douglas
A A M Duncan 1989: Scotland, The Making of the Kingdom, Edinburgh, Mercat Press

# 6

# After Carham

 ## Lothian: Lost and Found

Rivers like the Tweed form natural boundaries but, before modern states, there were no modern borders. A battle could extend the power and influence of the victor as against the loser; but this position could be reversed by the result of the next battle. The Scots may have been the dominant power in Lothian from 973 AD or earlier but, when Malcolm II tried to get the upper hand south of the Tweed by his siege of Durham in 1006, his exploit back-fired: he was defeated by Uhtred of Bamburgh and retreated to Scotland for more than a decade. The balance of power in Lothian shifted back towards Northumbria. When Malcolm II returned to the issue in 1018 he had Owain of Strathclyde as an ally and the new king of England, Cnut, was pre-occupied with southerly matters and Danish matters. Uhtred was weak and alone in Bamburgh. How opportune!

| Kings of England | | Kings of Scotland | |
|---|---|---|---|
| Cnut | 1016-1035 | 1005-1034 | Malcolm II |
| Harold 'Harefoot' | 1035-1040 | 1034-1040 | Duncan I |
| Harthacanute | 1040-1042 | | |
| Edward the 'Confessor' | 1042-1066 | 1040-1057 | Macbeth |

Malcolm was the victor at Carham: he had a long and successful reign until his death in 1034. Owain may have died in the battle. As Clarkson points out: 'If Owain the Bald had any further dealings with his neighbours after 1018, the sources fail to mention them. Nothing more is heard of him, not even the date of his death.' (Clarkson 2014: 143) Uhtred survived but not for long: he was killed shortly afterwards by Thurbrand, at the behest of Cnut.

Soon thereafter, Lothian was ceded by Eadwulf and then by Cnut:

> Upon his [Uhtred's] death, his brother Eadulf, surnamed Cudel, a lazy and
> cowardly fellow, succeeded him in the earldom. Apprehensive that the
> Scots would revenge upon himself the slaughter which his brother had
> inflicted upon them, as has already been mentioned [the siege of Durham
> of 1006 - see above], he yielded up to them the whole of Lothian, to
> soothe them and procure a peace; and hence it is that Lothian became
> added to the kingdom of Scotland. (Simeon 1865: 767)

Cnut had been crowned king of England in December 1016. Rodolfus Glaber, a
Burgundian chronicler of the late 1020s, records:

> After this also the same Cnut set out with a very great army to subdue to
> himself the nation of the Scots; whose king was called Malcolm, [and was]
> powerful in resources and arms, and (what was most efficacious) very
> Christian in faith and deed. And when [Malcolm] knew that Cnut
> audaciously sought to invade his kingdom, he collected his nation's whole
> army, and resisted him strongly, so that he should not succeed.

> And Cnut shamelessly prosecuted these claims for a long time, and
> vigorously; but at last, by persuasion of the aforesaid Richard, the duke
> of Rouen, and of [Richard's] sister [Emma, wife of Cnut] he entirely laid
> aside all ferocity, for the love of God; became gentle, and lived in peace.
> Moreover also for friendship's sake, having affection for the king of the
> Scots, he received [Malcolm's] son from the holy font of baptism.
> (Anderson 1922: 545-6)

Besides settling matters with Malcolm on the military and diplomatic fronts,
Cnut may also have been taking advantage of the opportunity to embellish his
Christian credentials. According to Higham 'It was probably on this occasion that
he [Cnut] came as a pilgrim to St Cuthbert's, ostentatiously approaching the
shrine on foot from Garmondsway and bestowing on the church substantial
estates in the vicinity.' (Higham 1993: 230)

In his authoritative account of the period Alex Woolf sums it up:

> It seems likely that Uhtred's removal provided a perfect opportunity for
> a face-saving agreement between the two kings and that Cnut was happy
> to cede the lands north of the Tweed in return for formal submission from
> Malcolm. (Woolf 2007: 239-40).

Malcolm II died in 1034 and Cnut in 1035. Malcolm left no sons and only one
daughter, Bethoc, so the new Scottish king was Duncan I (1034-1040), grandson

of Malcolm and son of Bethoc. Duncan followed his predecessors with a southerly raid in 1038 but, in a repeat of 1006, the Scots were beaten off at Durham. The defeat left Duncan discredited: he was killed and replaced by Macbeth (1040-1057). (In his play *Macbeth*, Shakespeare portrays Duncan as an old man but in fact he was probably still in his thirties at the time of his death). In England, Cnut was succeeded by his sons Harthacanute (1035-1040) and then Harold 'Harefoot' (1040-1042) before the Saxon line was restored with Edward the 'Confessor' (1042-1066).

Photo 4 - The Tweed near Carham with inquisitive Tweedside sheep curious as to the author's purpose.

Fig 3: Kings, 1018 to 'Canmore' and 'Conqueror'

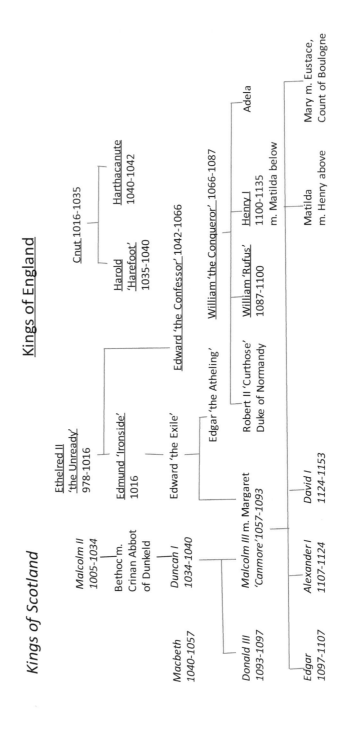

_Kings of Scotland_

Malcolm II
1005-1034

Bethoc m.
Crinan Abbot
of Dunkeld

Duncan I
1034-1040

Macbeth
1040-1057

Malcolm III m. Margaret
'Canmore'1057-1093

Donald III
1093-1097

Edgar
1097-1107

Alexander I
1107-1124

David I
1124-1153

Kings of England

Ethelred II
'the Unready'
978-1016

Cnut 1016-1035

Harold
'Harefoot'
1035-1040

Harthacanute
1040-1042

Edmund 'Ironside'
1016

Edward 'the Confessor' 1042-1066

Edward 'the Exile'

Edgar 'the Atheling'

William 'the Conqueror' 1066-1087

Robert II 'Curthose'
Duke of Normandy

William 'Rufus'
1087-1100

Henry I
1100-1135
m. Matilda below

Adela

Matilda
m. Henry above

Mary m. Eustace,
Count of Boulogne

# 7

# The Norman Effect

## Conqueror & sons
## vs. Canmore & sons

In 1054, Siward, Earl of Northumbria, intervened against Macbeth in support of Malcolm 'Canmore' (son of Duncan I). Macbeth lost at Dunsinane and Malcolm became Lord of Lothian and Strathclyde, the two border territories. In 1057, Malcolm killed Macbeth at Lumphanan, Aberdeenshire, and became king Malcolm III.

| Kings of England | | Kings of Scotland | |
|---|---|---|---|
| Edward the 'Confessor' | 1042-1066 | 1040-1057 | Macbeth |
| Harold II 'Godwinson' | 1066-1066 | 1057-1093* | Malcolm III 'Canmore' |
| William I the 'Conqueror' | 1066-1087 | | |

\* King Lulach, for a few months in 1058

## Malcolm's First Invasion 1061 AD

Having supported Malcolm, Siward may have been expecting peace on his northern border, but in 1061 Malcolm raided Lindisfarne and north Northumbria and captured Cumberland, the first of his five military expeditions to the south: 1061, 1070, 1079, 1091 and 1093. These were incursions across the border of the Tweed but not necessarily into England; in the first instance, these were incursions into what remained of Northumbria.

In 1057 Edward the Exile returned from Hungary but died in suspicious circumstances one week later leaving his two-year old son Edgar the Atheling as the only male heir-apparent of the Saxon bloodline (see Box: Margaret of

Scotland). When Edward the Confessor died on 5 January 1066, Edgar was still only eleven; too young to claim the throne. Harold Godwinson was declared king of England, but this merely triggered action by bigger powers. Harold 'Hardrada', the Norse king, invaded from the north and William the 'Bastard', the Norman, invaded from the south. Godwinson defeated Hardrada at Stamford Bridge (Map 5) on 25 September but on 14 October, only three weeks later, lost to the Normans at the battle of Hastings. William became king of England at Westminster on Christmas Day 1066 by right of conquest.

Much has been written about the Norman Conquest of Britain. I will not repeat here all the details from William Kapelle's excellent account in "The Norman Conquest of the North" (Kapelle 1979). A few incidents are enough to give the flavour:

- In 1067 William appointed Copsig as Earl of Northumbria but he was beheaded by the locals only a few weeks later.

- William then appointed Gospatrick (of Bamburgh) but he joined in a rebellion with the Mercians, which failed, and fled to Scotland.

- In 1068 William took York and ordered the building of a castle. He appointed Robert Comines as Earl of Northumbria.

- Comines took Durham on 30 January 1069 but the following day he and his 700 troops were slain by the locals.

- In the winter of 1069-70 William carried out the 'Harrying of the North'.

## The Harrying of the North

The 'harrying' was a wholesale destruction of people, buildings, farms and livestock: a devastation with the apparent purpose of turning the north, particularly Yorkshire, into a desert. Lothian was "a natural asylum for the Northumbrians hustled away by the attacks of William the Conqueror and the harrying of the north" (Poole 1955: 265).

# Malcolm's Second Invasion 1070 AD

Presumably Malcolm of Scotland thought that he and William the Conqueror could divide the north of England between them. In 1070, within months of the harrying, Malcolm invaded Cumbria and then moved east to Cleveland, Hartlepool and Monk-wearmouth (Map 5). An unexpected consequence was that 'on his second raid into Gospatrick's earldom [Northumbria] he found himself at Wearmouth and there, on the beach, he met a girl.' (Woolf 2007: 271) Malcolm's first wife had been Ingibiorg (either the widow or the daughter of Thorfinn, Earl of Orkney). Margaret, the girl on the beach, would become his second wife: the mother of three kings of Scotland and a queen of England (see Box: Margaret of Scotland).

## Abernethy

William responded by sending an army north with naval support. Malcolm avoided military conflict and instead met William for discussions at Abernethy in 1072 (Map 5). Malcolm agreed to do homage to William, give up his son Duncan (son of Ingibiorg) as a hostage and expel from Scotland Margaret's brother Edgar 'the Atheling' together with Gospatrick, Earl of Bamburgh and their followers. They went to Flanders.

# Malcolm's Third Invasion 1079 AD

The peace agreed at Abernethy lasted until 1079, when Malcolm invaded Northumbria again. William responded by sending his son, Robert 'Curthose', north with an army. Malcolm avoided a military engagement but met Robert at Falkirk (Map 5) where the terms of the Abernethy agreement were renewed. In 1080, on his journey south, Robert initiated the building of a 'new castle' on the Tyne (Map 5). The impression given is that Abernethy and Falkirk had both been attempts by the Normans to intimidate Malcolm rather than to defeat him and the 'new castle upon Tyne' suggests that William still took the view that his defensive line could not yet be drawn on the Tweed. In a sense, in 1080, the border was on the Tyne.

## Domesday Book

William proceeded to consolidate his position. In 1085 he commenced the compilation of that tremendous work of data collection, the Domesday Book, which, according to the Anglo-Saxon Chronicle, records 'How many hundreds of hides were in the shire, what land the king himself had, and what stock upon the land; or, what dues he ought to have by the year from the shire.' However, the Domesday Book contains no data about anywhere in Scotland, Northumberland, Cumberland or Durham. In a sense, in 1085, the border was on the Tees.

## Margaret of Scotland: Queen and Saint

Margaret's husband King Malcolm and their eight children, including a queen of England and three kings of Scots, feature in this chapter and the next. Who was Margaret?

When Edmund Ironside died in 1016 he left two infant sons, Edmund and Edward (probably born posthumously). In flight from King Cnut they were whisked to safety in Sweden. Subsequently, they were taken further by a traditional Viking route on the rivers of Russia to the court of Yaroslav the Wise in Kiev. There they met Prince Andrew of Hungary and assisted him on his campaign to retake the throne of Hungary in 1046. Andrew gave them lands in southern Hungary at Mecsek-Nadasd, near Pecs.

Edward the Confessor, the king of England (1042-1066), had no sons or brothers and everyone could see that a succession crisis loomed. A possible solution was to recall his grand-nephew Edward from Hungary. Bishop Ealdred of Worcester's mission took three years. In August 1057, after forty years away, Edward returned to England as Edward the Exile. He died one week later, in suspicious circumstances. His son Edgar the Atheling was two years old and his daughters Margaret and Christina were both probably under ten years old. Together with their mother, Agatha, they were taken into the court of the Confessor and brought up as royal children. (Ronay 1989: 143).

In 1070, this time in flight from the Conqueror, their ship stopped at Wearmouth where they encountered King Malcolm III of Scots. He took in the remnants of the Saxon royal family and gave them refuge from the Normans in Scotland. Malcolm married Margaret 'not later than 1071' (Duncan 1975: 119). They had eight children of whom one became Queen Matilda of England and three became kings of Scots: Edgar 1097-1107, Alexander (1107-1124) and David (1124-1153). Margaret was canonised by Pope Innocent IV in 1250.

In 2010 my wife and I visited a small shrine to Margaret in the village church in Mecsek-Nadasd with her Hungarian cousin Ervin, who lived there.

| Kings of England | | Kings of Scotland | |
|---|---|---|---|
| William I the 'Conqueror' | 1066-1087 | 1057-1093* | Malcolm III 'Canmore' |
| William 'Rufus' | 1087-1100 | 1093-1097** | Donald III |

*King Lulach for a few months in 1058

**King Duncan II, for a few months in 1094

# Malcolm's Fourth Invasion 1091 AD

When William I died in 1087 his middle son William II 'Rufus' became king whilst his eldest son, Robert, remained across the Channel as Duke of Normandy. In 1091 Malcolm III invaded Northumbria as far as Chester-le-Street. In response, Rufus and Robert and their younger brother Henry jointly led an army into Scotland where Malcolm again made his peace, but it seems that William 'Rufus' (and his brothers?), had devised a strategy for the north. If his father William had conquered England up to and including Yorkshire, 'Rufus' would take the next step; he would take Cumbria.

## Cumbria

In 1092 William Rufus 'drove Dolfin, son of the Northumbrian earl Gospatrick, from Cumbria, capturing Carlisle (Map 5), the western doorway into Scotland, which he rebuilt and fortified with a castle, and where he planted a colony of rustics imported, it is said, from the southern parts of England. The English frontier was, as a result, advanced to the Tweed-Cheviot line.' (Poole 1955: 266)

# Malcolm's Final Invasion 1093 AD

Malcolm responded with his fifth attack south but he and Edward, his eldest son by Margaret, were defeated and killed at Alnwick by the earl of Northumberland on 13 November 1093 (Map 4). Queen Margaret died within days of receiving the news. It might have been expected that the new Scots king would be her next son Edgar, but there were two other candidates: Donald, Malcolm's brother, and Duncan, Malcolm's son by his first wife, Ingibiorg, who had been resident at the Anglo-Norman court since the agreement at Abernethy in 1072. The Scots '[---] chose Donald to be king, and expelled the English who had been 'with' his brother Malcolm, among them probably all the surviving sons of Margaret.' (Duncan 1975: 125)

## Norman Strategy

The English king, William Rufus, sensed an opportunity; he backed Duncan with an army. Duncan gained the throne for a few months but was killed on 12 November 1094 and Donald was king again. On the one side, Donald seems to have formed a triple alliance with Edgar's younger brother Edmund and with Gospatrick, the rebel earl of Northumberland. On the other side, Edgar gained backing from both the Norman king of England, William Rufus, and the Saxon, Edgar the 'Atheling': necessity can make strange bedfellows. Edgar defeated Donald in pitched battle and became Edgar, King of Scots, in 1097.

In the tenth century Yorkshire had been heavily Danish and Norse, with a clear sense of separateness from the Anglo-Saxons to the south. Cnut (1016-1035), a Danish king of England, had united Yorkshire with England south of the Humber but the north resisted the Normans. William the Conqueror carried out his 'harrying' and, whether as a desert or as a colony, by the 1080s he had moved the Anglo-Norman border north to include Yorkshire. In the 1090s William Rufus moved it further north to include Cumbria. The 'Harrying of the North' had taken a single season, mainly in Yorkshire, but the Norman campaign for control of Northumberland would take four decades.

The Normans seem to have had two strategies: first, to weaken the Scots kings by taking sides between them, leaving the winner beholden; and second, to strengthen their grip on Northumberland with more castles (see Box: Norman Castles in Northumberland).

## Simeon's Echoes

It appears that Simeon of Durham died in 1129. Most of his writing was probably done during the reign of King Henry I of England (1100-1135). Simeon may have noticed that the border conflicts of a previous age about which he was writing had their echo in the border conflicts of his own time through which he was living.

## Norman Castles in Northumberland

'In the years immediately following the Conquest it was essential that the castle should be erected quickly; the situation was potentially very hazardous since the Normans were in a rebellious countryside which might arise against them at any time. The [Norman] castle had to be simple and capable of being erected very quickly and, almost invariably, the earliest Norman castles were of the motte and bailey type. They were scattered over the countryside at strategic points, and at least one hundred were erected in the first half century. With the aid of pressed peasantry, a deep circular ditch was dug and the excavated earth thrown into the centre to form a mound, the "motte"; the top of this was flattened and on it was erected a simple wooden palisade.' (Wilkinson 1973: 7)

The 'new castle' upon Tyne (1080) was followed in the late eleventh century by castles at Prudhoe and Bywell, just upstream; Morpeth and Mitford, just up the modern A1; Alnwick, protecting the coastal route, and Elsdon, protecting the Redesdale route (the modern A68). These castles gave protection against occasional Scottish incursion but their everyday purpose was to dominate the territory of Northumberland; they were castles of occupation as well as defence. (see also Barrow 1973: 146-7)

By the 1120s, Henry had commanded Walter Espec, a Norman baron of Yorkshire, and Rannulf Flambard, the Norman bishop of Durham, to build castles on the Tweed at Wark and Norham respectively. The timing of the construction of the castles at Callaly, Harbottle, Warkworth and Wooler is not so clear but all four are of motte and bailey construction: Harbottle was "built circa 1157 by the Umfraville family for their centre of operations" (Wilkinson 1973: 87) and Warkworth was "captured by the Scots in 1173" (Wilkinson 1973: 178). Their location suggests that these four were probably commenced in the early 12th century as the Norman's gradually extended their grip further north.

Berwick Castle is of similar vintage but on the north bank of the Tweed. According to the website www.castlesfortsbattles.co.uk it "was built by David I of Scotland no later than 1127 [---]". Berwick town and castle changed hands frequently.

| Kings of England | | Kings of Scotland | |
|---|---|---|---|
| Henry I | 1100-1135 | 1097-1107 | Edgar I |
| | | 1107-1124 | Alexander I |
| Stephen I | 1135-1154 | 1124-1153 | David I |

# Edgar, Alexander and David

William Rufus was killed in 1100 AD.[1] He was succeeded by his brother Henry who married a Scottish princess, Matilda (a daughter of Malcolm and Margaret known in Scotland as Edith). As Queen Matilda she granted her interest in Carham to the monks of St Cuthbert at Durham: her husband, King Henry, later granted Carham to Walter Espec (see Addendum Carham: The Church). Of Matilda's six brothers, three became successive kings of Scots: Edgar (1097-1107), Alexander (1107-1124) and David (1124-1153).

William Rufus had assisted Edgar to the throne of Scotland. 'The reign of Edgar was a period of peaceful development interrupted only by the Norwegian conquest of the western isles. His brother Alexander [his successor] lived and ruled chiefly in the country north of the Firth of Forth leaving, according to a plan arranged by Edgar, the more anglicized districts of Lothian and Cumbria to his brother David.' (Poole 1955: 268)

This may have been Edgar's plan, but when Alexander became king in 1107, he seemed reluctant to follow it. David turned to the English king Henry (and perhaps to his sister, Matilda) to put pressure on Alexander to grant him the southern earldoms of Lothian and Strathclyde: Alexander conceded in 1113 (Oram 2008: 61). Henry played a canny hand. He was married to Matilda and supporting one of her brothers (David) to run a buffer state in southern Scotland which kept the other brother (Alexander, King of Scots) away from Northumbria.

---

[1] Rufus was killed by an arrow on 2 August 1100 whilst out hunting at Brockenhurst, Hampshire. His younger brother Henry, one of the hunting party, rushed immediately to Winchester where he seized the royal Treasury, buried his brother, held an impromptu council and proceeded to London where, only three days later, he was crowned King Henry I in Westminster Abbey by the bishop of London on 5 August. No-one was ever brought to justice for the killing of William Rufus. (Chambers 1981: 117)

In a sense, from 1113 to 1124, the border was on the Forth, or perhaps the Lammermuirs (Map 5).

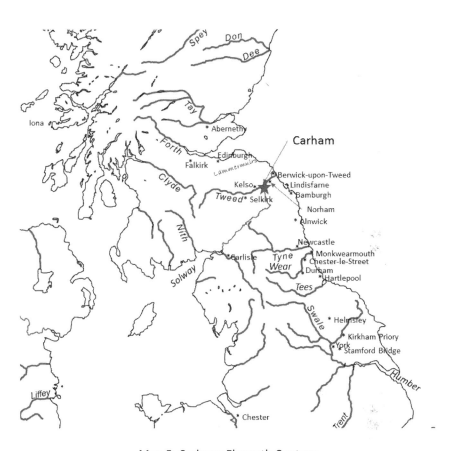

Map 5: Carham: Eleventh Century

# The 'Quietus' of Henry I and David I

As the youngest of six brothers there had been little or no expectation that David would ever become king. He had been brought up largely in England and France as an Anglo-Norman knight at the Anglo-Norman court where he was known as 'the Queen's brother' and he was on friendly personal terms with Henry I, King of England. Through his marriage in 1113 to Matilda, Countess of Northampton (widow of Simon de Senlis) he was a substantial baron of England with title to key territories south of the Tweed. Matilda's parents were Waltheof, Earl of Northumbria, and Judith, Countess of Huntingdon and Northampton. Waltheof's father was Siward, Earl of Northumbria (1041-1055) and his mother Elfleda was the daughter of Ealdred, Earl of Northumbria. Ealdred's father had been Uhtred, the loser at Carham. Accordingly, in his marriage, David acquired not only the substantial midlands earldom of Huntingdon and Northampton but also a claim to the lands of Northumbria, the lands of Uhtred.

During his period as an Earl of the border country from 1113 David introduced Norman monks to southern Scotland and built several border abbeys. The first was the Tironensian abbey of Selkirk in 1113 which he transferred to Kelso, only five miles from Carham, in 1128 (Map 4). After becoming king in 1124 he used his early years to extend the power of the Scottish throne.

> By 1136, therefore, David had achieved an unprecedented mastery of mainland Scotland. Direct royal authority had been imposed over the whole of the Southern Uplands except for Fergus' domain in Galloway, while north of the Forth royal power was entrenched firmly from the Moray firthlands to Argyll, Fife to Buchan. Outwith that expanded core, the still notionally independent rulers of Galloway, Orkney, Caithness and the Isles had been brought into his orbit, and David's influence extended from Man to the northern Isles. (Oram 2008: 119)

David had good reason to try to extend his influence further by bringing his wife's lands in Northumbria within the Scottish kingdom but, for the moment, he bided his time and consolidated his position in Scotland. The position changed in 1135.

Figure 4: Kings, from 'Canmore' and 'Conqueror' to 1249 AD

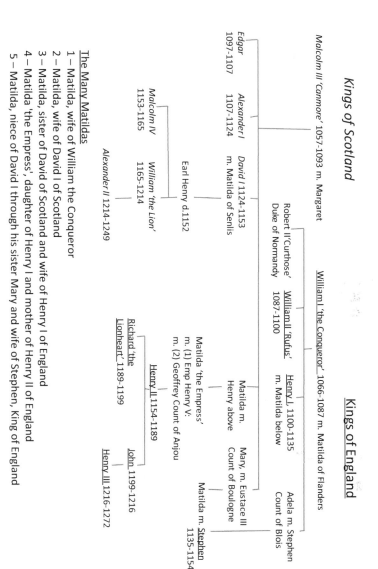

The Many Matildas

1 – Matilda, wife of William the Conqueror
2 – Matilda, wife of David I of Scotland
3 – Matilda, sister of David of Scotland and wife of Henry I of England
4 – Matilda 'the Empress', daughter of Henry I and mother of Henry II of England
5 – Matilda, niece of David I through his sister Mary and wife of Stephen, King of England

# 8

# Win - Lose - Draw

 ## High Stakes Poker

## David I Wins Northumbria 1135 AD

On the death of Henry I in 1135, his nephew Stephen of Blois became king of England. Stephen was married to Matilda, niece of King David. However, Stephen was challenged by Henry's daughter Matilda 'the Empress', another niece of King David (see Figure 4). England descended into civil war. David took advantage. 'According to Richard of Hexham, David's initial operation met with considerable success, capturing Carlisle, Wark, Alnwick, Norham and Newcastle, although the symbolic fortress of Bamburgh remained in the possession of Stephen's supporters.' (Oram 2008: 122) David advanced to Durham where he encountered Stephen's forces.

### Treaty of Durham 1136

Instead of fighting, the two negotiated the Treaty of Durham of 1136. David returned Newcastle to Stephen but retained Carlisle and Huntingdon in the name of his son, Prince Henry and, "[-—] under an agreement made with King Stephen at Durham in February [1136] restored the border [of Cumbria] to the Rere Cross on Stainmore" (Barrow 1973: 147)

David claimed that his interventions in the north of England were in support of his niece Matilda 'the Empress' but his actions in 1138 suggest that his real motive was to gain territory for his Scots kingdom.

> "The invasion of Northumberland began on 10 January 1138 when William fitz Duncan led a Scottish force down the river Tweed, probably from Roxburgh, to besiege Walter Espec's castle at Wark-on-Tweed, which was held by Walter's nephew Jordan de Bussey. The castle, which controlled a strategic crossing of the river as well as the land routes along the south side of the valley between the river and the northern spur of

the Pennines, was the key to Scottish control of north-west Northumberland." (Oram 2008: 129)

David's forces had a victory west of the Pennines at Clitheroe on 10 June and Stephen's forces prevailed on 22 August, at the Battle of the Standard, near Northallerton, but neither victory was decisive. The struggle continued.

## Treaty of Durham 1139

Alberic, Cardinal bishop of Ostia, legate of Pope Innocent II, was in the country for other reasons but he met with David at Carlisle on 26 September and may have engaged in some shuttle diplomacy between the two kings over the winter. On 9 April 1139 Matilda, the Queen of England, met her uncle, king David of Scotland, at Durham and the pair settled an agreement; the second Treaty of Durham.

> "Stephen yielded up to Earl Henry the earldom of Northumberland, excepting Bamburgh and Newcastle, in lieu of which he was awarded land of equivalent value in southern England, and the lands of St Cuthbert around Norham and the properties of Hexham. [-—] Earl Henry travelled south with his cousin [Queen Matilda] to meet with Stephen at Nottingham, where the treaty was approved and ratified by the king." (Oram 2008: 143)

David's son, Prince Henry had to do homage to king Stephen for these lands but, with Bamburgh and Newcastle surrounded by Scots forces, for all practical purposes, the border was on the Tyne. In a sense, in the west, the border was on the Ribble.

David pushed on. By 1141 'The western side of England to a line parallel with the Humber estuary was firmly in Scottish hands and, to emphasise how David viewed his possession of this land, he issued the charters in respect of it in his capacity as King of Scots with no reference to any overriding authority of the English crown.' (Oram 2008: 179) In a sense, the border in the west was now on the Mersey.

The pinnacle of David's ambition came in 1149. King Stephen opposed the appointment of Henry Murdac as Archbishop of York. David decided to support Murdac in alliance with Ranulf, earl of Chester, and the teenage Prince Henry of Anjou, who had been at Carlisle earlier in the year to be knighted by David. However, King Stephen pre-empted their plan by occupying York. Neither side felt strong enough to rout the other. David stood down and Stephen stood down and York stood still. In effect, the border in the east was still on the Tyne, but with the bishop of Durham and the lands of St Cuthbert as a kind of buffer state in the lands between the Tyne and the Tees.

David's approach at this time suggested that his ambition was to take all the lands north of the Humber. He spent much of his reign living in the border country in Roxburgh (only six miles from Carham) and Carlisle, the town colonized by Rufus as recently as 1092. It appears to have been David's intention that his son Henry would succeed him as king of Scotland and bring with him the lands of Northumbria. The great tragedy for David is that Prince Henry predeceased him, dying in 1152.

Prince Henry left three sons. David arranged that the eldest, ten-year old Malcolm, be taken around Scotland by Duncan, the Earl of Fife, to be displayed to the people as their future king. He himself took the nine-year old William to Newcastle for the people to see their future earl (Oram 2008: 201). King David died at Carlisle on 29 May 1153, only ten months after Prince Henry. Henry's three sons became King Malcolm IV (1153-1165), King William I, nicknamed 'The Lion' (1165-1214) and David, Earl of Huntingdon.[1] In a sense, from 1135 to 1153, the eastern border had been on the Tyne and sometimes the Tees.

| Kings of England | | Kings of Scotland | |
|---|---|---|---|
| Stephen I | 1135-1154 | 1124-1153 | David I |
| Henry II | 1154-1189 | 1153-1165 | Malcolm IV 'the Maiden' |
| Richard I 'Lionheart' | 1189-1199 | 1165-1214 | William I 'the Lion' |
| John | 1199-1216 | | |

---

[1] David, Earl of Huntingdon, never became king but he became a key dynastic link in the Scottish monarchy. In 1291 and 1292, when the fourteen 'Competitors' for the throne of Scotland argued their case before Edward I of England at Norham Castle, the claims of the two leading contenders were both based on their descent from David. John Balliol was the grandson of Earl David's eldest daughter Margaret, and Robert Bruce was the son of Earl David's second daughter Isobel. Robert the Bruce, who became King of Scotland on 25 March 1306, was the grandson of Robert Bruce 'the Competitor'.

Under the peace settlement of England's bitter civil wars, on the death of King Stephen, on 25 October 1154, Henry of Anjou took the throne as King Henry II, England's first Angevin monarch. In the same year he formally abolished the Earldom of York, taking it upon himself, and appointed King Stephen's nephew, Hugh de Puiset as bishop of Durham.

# Malcolm IV Loses Northumbria 1157 AD

In July 1157 King Henry met with King Malcolm at Chester. Malcolm, aged about sixteen, was a weak character with a mis-shapen head, probably the result of Paget's disease.[2] He was known as Malcolm 'the Fair' and later as 'the Maiden'. In contrast, the twenty-four-year-old Henry was a well-educated and worldly-wise knight at the height of his powers. Duncan's summary quotes William of Newburgh and then the Chronicle of Melrose.

He [Malcolm] was asked to resign them [the northern districts] and '[-—] prudently judging that in this matter the king of England had the better of the case because of the strength of his resources' he yielded them up.

> [-—] Malcolm IV then did homage 'as his grandfather had been the vassal of the old King Henry saving all his dignities' and received the earldom of Huntingdon, now taken away from the luckless Simon de Senlis (Duncan 1975: 224).

This very precise wording means that homage was done for Huntingdon only. No-one had done homage for Scotland and only Prince Henry, Malcolm's father, for Northumbria. Perhaps expecting an adverse reaction in Scotland, Henry II 'began the reconstruction of Wark Castle and commanded Hugh, Bishop of Durham, to refortify Norham Castle.' (Duncan 1975 p 225) Malcolm's brother and heir-apparent, William the Lion, was furious. His father, Prince Henry, had been Earl of Cumbria and Northumberland and he had expected the same. As far as William was concerned, it was his Earldoms that Malcolm had conceded. As far as King Henry of England was concerned, in 1157, the border was back on the Tweed.

---

[2] Professor Duncan suggests that the soubriquet 'Canmore', which means "big head" may have originated with Malcolm IV. Somehow, perhaps in error, later writers transferred the nick-name back to refer to Malcolm III, who is the one known as Malcolm 'Canmore' today. (Duncan 2002: 75)

# William the Lion Loses Scotland 1174 AD

When his brother Malcolm died in December 1165 William the Lion succeeded to the throne and sought opportunities to reclaim the northern districts. He seems to have raised the matter with Henry at Windsor in March 1166 and later the same year at a tournament at Mont St. Michel. Henry's second coronation ceremony was on 14 June 1170. A few days earlier he knighted William's younger brother David and, according to Fordun, William again raised the matter of Northumberland without success. These experiences may have led William to support a rebellion in 1173 by three sons of King Henry; namely young Henry (age 18), Richard (15) and Geoffrey (14). William invaded Northumbria in support of this rebellion, but he was caught and detained at Alnwick on 13 July 1174 and taken to Newcastle as a prisoner. He would pay dearly for this mistake.

## The Treaty of Falaise

'On 26 July 1174, King William was brought to Henry II at Northampton with his feet ignominiously shackled beneath the belly of his horse;' (Duncan 1975: 230). Northampton was the heart of the Earldom of Huntingdon. Being paraded there was not just a humiliation, it was an insult. William was then imprisoned in Falaise, Normandy. In England Henry and his sons agreed a peace on 30 September 1174. William was left with little option: on 8 December 1174 he signed the Treaty of Falaise.

> 'By this Treaty William of Scotland became the vassal of the king of England. There was no longer a doubt as to what this vassalage signified; the language is unequivocal: "for Scotland and all his other land". The Scottish church was to be subject to the church of England, [    ]    The five strongest castles of Scotland - those of Roxburgh, Berwick, Jedburgh, Edinburgh and Stirling - were surrendered into the king's hands, and a number of distinguished Scottish lords were given over as hostages.' (Poole 1955: 277)

King William's ignominy was long-lived. When Edward I of England presented his claim to lordship of Scotland in 1296 he quoted the Treaty of Falaise as one of his grounds (Duncan 2002: 222). Under the terms of the treaty William was released to return to Scotland but with one further humiliation:

> 'In August 1175, in the cathedral church of St Peter at York, King William and his brother [Earl David], followed by the prelates and magnates of Scotland, did homage (the prelates excepted) and swore fealty to Henry

II. He [Henry] relied upon the moral effect of that act to bind the kingdom of Scotland to himself.' (Duncan 1975: 231)

Henry II had not just taken Northumbria, he had now taken the whole of Scotland within his kingdom of England, binding William and the Scots nobles to himself. In 1174, the border was transcended.

Photo 5 - Carham: The village in March 2018

# The 'Quitclaim' of Canterbury 1189 AD

Richard I 'the Lionheart' became king of England after his father, Henry II, died at Chinon on 6 July 1189. Richard was desperate for money to go on Crusade. He met King William of Scotland at Canterbury on 5 December 1189. In what became known as the Quitclaim of Canterbury, Richard sold the Treaty of Falaise to William for ten thousand merks. According to Duncan, William:

> [-—] was released from 'all agreements which our good father Henry . . . exacted from him by new charters and by his capture so that he shall do to us . . . whatever his brother Malcolm, King of Scotland, did of right and ought to have done of right to our predecessors'. The allegiance of his vassals was restored to him and the document recorded that King William 'has become our liegeman for all the lands for which his predecessors were liegemen of our predecessors'. (Duncan 1975: 236)

Roger Howden, the busy clerk [—] was equally in no doubt of what the Quitclaim meant:

'. . . the king of Scots did him homage for the holding of his dignities in England [e.g. the Earldom of Northampton] as the kings of Scots his predecessors were accustomed to hold them . . . and King Richard . . . quit claimed him and all his heirs for ever. . . from all allegiance and subjection for the kingdom of Scotland.' (Duncan 1975: 237-8)

This was a reversion to the position in the time of Malcolm IV. It had taken William 15 years but, by courtesy of Richard's crusading zeal, he had regained his kingdom of Scotland as held by his brother. However, he had not yet regained the lands of Northumbria as held by his father. The border was back, and on the Tweed.

Map 6: Carham: Twelfth and Thirteenth Century

# 9

# A Settlement

## Treaty of 1237 and *Leges Marchiorum*

William made persistent attempts to regain the northern counties. For example, in 1194, King Richard was in Winchester for his second coronation.

> The kings met on 4 April and on the following day William asked for 'the dignities and honours which his predecessors had had in England. He also asked for the earldom of Northumbria, Cumberland, Westmorland and the "county" of Lancaster. (Duncan 1975: 239)

There was some diplomatic haggling, but no agreement was reached. King Richard departed for France on 22 April. They never met again. In Richard's absence from England on Crusade his brother John acted in his stead and, when Richard died in 1199, he took the throne substantively as King John (the King John of Magna Carta in 1215). John had several inconclusive diplomatic meetings with King William of Scotland on the matter of Cumbria and Northumbria. William kept trying to pin him down and John kept dodging the issue. Professor Duncan gives three examples:

- On 22 November 1200 William met John at Lincoln. 'His renewed demand for the three counties led to prolonged discussion, no agreement [-—]'

- '[-—] the two kings certainly met for four days of vain negotiations at York in February 1206.'

- 'In 1209 their affairs reached a crisis which has never been explained and were resolved by a treaty which has not survived.' (Duncan 1975: 241)

## The Peace of Norham 1209 AD

In 1205 the bishop of Durham had started to build a castle at Tweedmouth, across the river from Berwick. William the Lion had demolished it. 'The relations became more and more strained until in 1209 both countries prepared for war.

But when John appeared in August at the head of a large army at Norham, William capitulated.' (Poole 1955: 282) However, the castle at Tweedmouth was never built.

In 1209 William the Lion was almost seventy years old. In April King John proceeded from Alnwick to Norham. 'Evidently forewarned, William mustered an army at Roxburgh'. Various diplomatic exchanges took place, both sides were persuaded not to come to blows 'and on 7 August 1209, at Norham, William came to John's peace.' (Duncan 1975: 242-3) The border was still on the Tweed.

Unfortunately, no copies of the Peace of Norham survive. According to Professor Duncan: 'The documents of the treaty were returned to Scotland in 1237, or so the treaty of that year provided, and they were certainly not in London in the 1290s. Neither were they in Edinburgh, so the Scots had probably destroyed them, evidence of their disparaging character.' (Duncan 1975: 248)

After splicing together clues from the writings of Fordun, Bower, Wendover and others and from the terms of the Treaty of York (1237), Professor Duncan suggests that the Peace of Norham (1209) may have included:

- William giving up his claim to the northern counties as king of Scotland but accepting them as an appanage for his heir, his son Alexander;

- marriage arrangements between King William's two infant daughters, Margaret and Isobel, and King John's two baby sons, Henry (born October 1207) and Richard (born January 1209); and

- payment by William of 15,000 merks.

In this passage of his book, Professor Duncan's efforts to get a firm grasp of the facts seem to parallel King William's efforts to get a firm grasp of Northumbria. For both, there is a palpable sense of sand dribbling through fingers (Duncan 1975: 239-255).

When William of Scotland died on 4 December 1214, his sixteen-year-old son was enthroned at Scone as King Alexander II. In England King John was much preoccupied with rebellious barons and on Friday 19 June 2015 he affixed his seal to Magna Carta. However, that did not solve his problems on the Tweed.

> On 19 October 1215 the Scots laid siege to the castle of Norham [-—] for forty days. On 22 October the barons of Northumbria did homage to Alexander, and it is likely that the twenty-five English barons charged to

see the execution of the Great Charter had already adjudged the three northern counties to him. (Duncan 1975: 521)

In response:

> In December King John turned his attention to the north and on 4 January 1216 was at York. On 11 January the rebellious barons of Yorkshire, in fear of their king, did homage to Alexander II at Melrose. [-—] in mid-January King John entered Scotland, taking Berwick and advancing to Haddington and Dunbar. All three towns, together with Roxburgh, were burned within ten days without interference from King Alexander. (Duncan 1975: 522)

King John was making a point. In 1216, the border was still on the Tweed.

Prince Louis, heir to the crown of France, had decided that now would be a good time to press his claim to the throne of England, and so landed in Kent on 21 May 1216. On 8 August, Alexander took advantage of Louis' actions by taking Carlisle and then Barnard Castle and then proceeding to Dover to greet Louis. King John 'set out on his last campaign, the object of which was the recovery of his position in the eastern counties [East Anglia].' (Poole 1955: 485) He died at Newark on 19 October 1216. The death of King John reduced Louis' appeal and the English barons rallied round John's nine-year old son, Henry. It is notable that 'In the third week of December 1217, Alexander did homage to Henry III at Northampton for the earldom of Huntingdon [-—] and for the other lands (Tynedale) which he held of the English king.' (Duncan 1975: 524)

Meanwhile the Scots and the English had both been petitioning the Pope. The Papal legate Pandulph met Alexander II and the procurators of Henry III at Norham on 2 August and met both kings at York on 15 June 1220 to effect a settlement (Henry was now aged thirteen). The northern counties were not mentioned in the settlement which was mainly about marriages for Alexander and his two sisters. At York on 19 June 1221 King Alexander II of Scotland married Joan, eldest sister of King Henry III of England.

| Kings of England | | Kings of Scotland | |
|---|---|---|---|
| Henry III | 1216-1272 | 1214-1249 | Alexander II |
| | | 1249-1286 | Alexander III |

# The Treaty of York 1237 AD

The matter of the northern counties remained in suspense until April 1236 when Alexander and Henry met at Newcastle. Negotiations carried through to a further meeting at York which were facilitated by a further Papal legate, Otto. "For three days, in September 1237, the legate Otto conducted negotiations between the kings at York; on 25 September a treaty was sealed and the kings parted." (Duncan 1975: 533) In a sad post-script, after the meeting at York, Queen Joan went to Canterbury to visit the shrine of Thomas á Becket and died there on 4 March 1238.

Poole summarises the position of Alexander II:

> "His interventions in English affairs had gained him nothing. Carlisle, his one conquest, had to be surrendered in 1217; and twenty years later (1237) the claim to the northern counties, the aspiration of the kings of Scotland since the time of David I, was once and for all abandoned in return for a grant of English lands of the annual value of £200.* So closed the long contest. The frontier between the two kingdoms along the Tweed-Cheviot line which had been won by Rufus's conquest of Carlisle in 1092, lost in the troubles of the reign of Stephen, recovered by Henry II in 1157, and bitterly contested during the long reign of William the Lion, was now finally admitted by both nations." (Poole 1955: 283)

> * The lands granted were Wark [on Tyne] and Grindon in Northumberland; and Penrith, Scotby, Carlton, Langwathby, Salkeld, and Sowerby in Cumberland. (Poole 1955: 283)

Richard Lomas observes:

> To us it may be inconceivable that the Anglo-Scottish border should be other than where it is; but we must recognise that this is the result of nothing but long use. Between Northumberland on the one hand, and Berwickshire and Roxburghshire on the other, there were no significant differences of race, language and way of life at any level. [-—] In the end, it was the greater ability of the latter [the king of England] to enforce allegiance that finally determined that Northumberland would be an English county. (Lomas 1996: 33)

# The Laws of the Marches 1249 AD

The birth of the border was at Carham in 1018 but there was a gestation period of at least a hundred years before the birth and, for about two hundred years thereafter, a period of uncertainty about whether the border might end up in another place. From the time of the Quitclaim of Canterbury in 1189 it became gradually apparent that the border was likely to remain on the Tweed and when the two kings set their seals to the Treaty of York in 1237 the border *de facto* (in practice) became the border *de jure* (in law).

To regulate disputes about land and fishing and the procedures for dealing with fugitive outlaws and other border questions, a legal border needs a *Leges Marchiorum* (a set of Border Laws). Carham was a key venue:

> Less than a decade after the sealing of the Treaty of York, a squabble erupted between the canons of the little priory of Carham [Wark priory] and the Scotsman Bernard de Hadden, concerning lands claimed by both.

> At issue was the delineation of the "true and ancient marches" between the kingdoms, but overshadowing the dispute was the larger matter of jurisdiction in the settlement of cross-border grievances. In October 1245 Henry III dispatched the sheriff of Northumberland, Hugh de Bolebec, to Reddenburn, where arrangements were made to perambulate the territory and to determine the junction of the English lands belonging to Carham, and the Scottish lands claimed by Hadden. (Neville 1998: 1-5)

As Hugh de Bolebec's letter shows, this was not an instant success (See Box: Letter from Hugh de Bolebec). However, four years later '[-—] the codification of 1249 thus became the basis of a system of law that remained unique to the border lands throughout the later medieval period.' (Neville 1998: 1-5)

## Redden Burn and Duddo Burn

The border jury met at Redden Burn, the western boundary of the parish of Carham, adjacent to Hadden in the community of Sprouston in Scotland. The Duddo Burn is the eastern boundary of Carham parish, adjacent to Cornhill-on-Tweed, in ancient Norhamshire. The 'Laws of the Marches' of 14 April 1249 clarify an important role for both tiny streams. In the event of any matter concerning the Border laws, those arising between Duddo (spelled 'Dedey' in the original) 'and the sea' answered their charges at Hamisford (modern Norham) and those arising 'above Dedey' (modern Carham) answered at the Redden Burn. In a sense,

Carham had been the venue for battle (1018) and it was now a venue for settlement (1249).

## Letter from Hugh de Bolebec of Bywell, Sheriff of Northumberland, to Henry III, King of England

"I and the knights of Northumberland met the Justiciar of Lothian, David Lindsay, the earl of Dunbar, and many other Scottish knights at Reddenburn. Six English and six Scottish knights were elected as a jury to make a true perambulation of the march between the two kingdoms, and in particular between the lands of Carham (in England) and Hadden (in Scotland).

The six English knights, with one accord, immediately set off along the rightful and ancient marches between the two kingdoms, but the Scottish knights entirely disagreed and contradicted them. I and the Justiciar of Lothian thereupon decided to elect a second jury to reinforce the first. Once again, the English knights agreed on the boundary and the Scots dissented.

Since the Scots had thus obstructed the business, I took it upon myself to empanel a third jury, this time of twenty-four English knights, who declared the true and ancient marches on oath. But when they started to make a perambulation of this line, the Justiciar and his fellow-Scots forcibly prevented them, and stopped them carrying out the perambulation by threats." (Barrow 1973: 156)

Photo 6: The border on the Redden Burn. To take this photograph the author
stood astride the burn with one foot in Scotland and one in England

# Appendix

 ## Carham: The Place

The earliest surviving reference to Carham is in the Historia De Sancto Cuthberto (HSC). Most of the HSC was written in about 945 AD in the church of St Cuthbert in Chester-le-Street (Simpson 1989: 397). It is primarily an account of the acquisition of lands by that church when they were at Lindisfarne and subsequently. Chapter 7 of the HSC, given below in Latin and in a modern English translation by Ted Johnson South, explains how St. Cuthbert acquired Carham:

> *7. Ea tempestate pugnauit Ecgfrid rex contra regem Merciorum Wulfhere filium Pendici, et ceso exercitu illius ipsum uicit et in fugam uno tantum comitante puerulo conuertit. Et hoc obtinuit per auxilium sancti Wilfridi, qui cum eo fuit, maxime uero per orationes sancti Cuthberti qui absens erat. Post hoc bellum dedit Ecgfrith rex sancto Cuthberto Carrum et quicquid ad eam pertinet, et habuit eum in summa ueneratione quam diu uixit, ipse et tota sua cognation, donec eo defuncto uenerunt Scaldingi et Eboracum ciuitatum fregerunt et terram ustauerunt. (South 2002: 48)*

> 7. In that time King Ecgfrith fought against the king of the Mercians, Wulfhere son of Penda, and having cut down [his] army he vanquished him and put him to flight with only one small boy accompanying [him]. And he [i.e. Ecgfrith] obtained this through the aid of St. Wilfrid, who was with him, but especially through the prayers of St Cuthbert, who was absent. After this battle King Ecgfrith gave Carham and whatever pertains to it to St Cuthbert and held him in the highest veneration as long as he lived, himself and all his kindred, until after his death the Scaldings [Danes] came and crushed York and devastated the land. (South 2002: 49)

We know that in 674 AD Wulfhere, king of the Mercians, attacked Northumbria 'at the head of an army drawn from all the southern English peoples. He was defeated by Ecgfrith, Oswiu's son, and the confederation which he had formed was dissolved.' (Stenton 1971: 85) We also know that on 28 March 685 AD

Cuthbert was consecrated bishop of Hexham, and subsequently Lindisfarne, but only after being pressed by King Ecgfrith. Thus, we know that King Ecgfrith was a great admirer of Cuthbert. This is Bede's account of the king's pleadings:

> Not long afterwards, when no small synod had gathered together, in the presence of the most pious king Ecgfrith beloved of God over which archbishop Theodore of blessed memory presided, he [Cuthbert] was elected to the bishopric of the church at Lindisfarne with the unanimous consent of all. And when he could by no means be dragged from his place by the many messengers and letters that were sent to him, at length this same king himself, together with most Holy Bishop Trumwine, as well as many other religious and powerful men, sailed to the island [Cuthbert's hermitage on Inner Farne]; they all knelt down and adjured him in the name of the Lord, with tears and prayers, until at last they drew him, also shedding many tears, from his sweet retirement and led him to the synod. When he had come in spite of his reluctance he was overcome by the unanimous will of them all and compelled to submit his neck to the yoke of the bishopric. His consecration however, was not carried out until after the end of that winter which was then beginning. (VSCB: Chapter XXIV)

It appears that in 1018 the patrimony of St Cuthbert included some lands which are now north of the border (e.g. Coldinghamshire, now part of East Lothian) and some which are now south of the border (e.g. Islandshire, Norhamshire and Carham). Islandshire is the coastal area north from Lindisfarne and then upstream along the south bank of the Tweed to Horncliffe; Norhamshire is the south bank of the Tweed from Horncliffe to Cornhill; Carham is the south bank of the Tweed from the Duddo Burn at Cornhill to Redden Burn. Evidence that these ancient shires pre-date the Anglo-Scottish border is provided by the adjacent Yetholmshire, now split with some parts in Scotland (e.g. Clifton, Halterburn, Yetholm) and some in England (e.g. Mindrum and Shotton) (Barrow 1973: 33).

# Carham: The Church

The Glendale Church Trail leaflet says of the Carham parish church: 'In 675 AD, St Cuthbert founded a small abbey here.' The *Historia De Sancto Cuthberto* (HSC) of 945 AD refers to Carham in 675 AD, but it does not mention a church. The HSC mentions 'Carham and whatever pertains to it (*Carrum et quicquid ad eam pertinet*).' As Max Adams clarifies, 'Names like Carham are those of vills or townships; that is to say, territorial units whose dependent settlements owed them food renders and services. [---] Whatever pertained to Carham in 675 looks as though it were at least a half-sized estate consisting of about six vills or townships.' (Adams 2014: 344) It would be surprising if there had been a church or an abbey of St Cuthbert in Carham in 675 or in 945 and the HSC had failed to mention it. The earliest record of a church in Carham is in the early twelfth century.

In a precept issued by Queen Matilda from Windsor one April between 1107 and 1116 she 'granted to St Cuthbert and his monks, the church of Carham and whatever pertains to it, in alms, so far as pertains to her; for the salvation of her husband and children and for herself and for the souls of her own and the King's parents.' (Johnson 1956: Calendar 1143)

In a notification of 1126 from Rockingham King Henry I confirmed Walter Espec's gift of several lands to the church of Kirkham including: 'the church of Carham, the church of Kirknewton (*Niwetona in Glendala*), the church in Ilderton, the vill of Titlington [in Eglingham], the houses of Ulchill the clerk in Carham and all his land, with the services which he rendered to Walter Espec (co, Northumb.)' (Johnson 1956: Calendar 1459)

The sparse language of the charters does not reveal what prompted Queen Matilda to confirm the church of Carham to the monks of St Cuthbert at Durham cathedral or what prompted her husband King Henry, a few years later, to grant the parish of Carham to Walter Espec and then to confirm Walter's grant of Carham church to the priory of Kirkham. However, it was in the 1120s that King Henry's policy of building castles in Northumberland reached the Tweed. The bishop of Durham was in possession of Coldinghamshire, well north of the Tweed, and Islandshire and Norhamshire on the Tweed's south bank. The bishop built Norham castle. It may be that King Henry was reluctant to put the whole of the Tweed border under the control of the bishop so he intruded Espec into Carham. Espec built Wark castle in the parish of Carham and shared border duties with the bishop.

Carham remained within the patrimony of St Cuthbert until granted to Walter Espec by King Henry in the 1120s. A century previously, in 1018 or 1019, Simeon reports that the news of the battle of Carham caused bishop Aldun to die of a broken heart (Simeon 1865: 675). From the bishop of Durham's point of view, in 1018, the people of Carham were 'people of St Cuthbert'.

Thus, a question remains. The charter of Queen Matilda granting 'the church of Carham and whatever pertains thereto' to the monks of St Cuthbert is the earliest reference to a church at Carham. The fact that the church is not next to the castle at Wark, but two miles west in the hamlet of Carham, suggests that the church may have been built before the castle. Carham parish church may have been on its present site before Queen Matilda and it may have been there before 1018 and it may have been there for decades or centuries before 1018. (see Box: St Cuthbert's Church in Carham)

---

### St Cuthbert's Church in Carham

St Cuthbert's church in Carham dates from 1790. The west tower, chancel and vestry were added in the 1860s. It is known that there was an earlier church on the same site in the 16th century.

The 6-inch OS Map of 1895 shows a "Monastery (Site of)" between the banks of the River Tweed and the present parish church. The surface looks like rough tufted grass, but the uneven ground suggests that there may have been building foundations at some point in the past. This site has not yet had the benefit of archaeological examination.

---

Walter Espec, of Helmsley in North Yorkshire, was one of the great Norman barons. He founded the Cistercian Rievaulx Abbey two miles from Helmsley as well as the Augustinian Kirkham Priory fifteen miles south of Helmsley towards York (Map 5). He built up Wark castle in the parish of Carham as an instrument of his feudal dominance of the surrounding land and as a defence against the Scots.

# Rannulf Flambard

In 1093 work started at Durham on a new cathedral. In 1099 William Rufus appointed Rannulf Flambard as bishop of Durham. Poole observes of Flambard that 'just before [William] the king's death he received the bishopric of Durham (1099), which he so shamefully abused that Henry I had to take it under his special protection.' Henry's charter of protection to the monks of Durham was granted 'on account of the injuries and violence which Rannulf the bishop did to them in his lifetime' (Poole 1955: 171, n).

Flambard became one of the first prisoners in the new Norman Tower of London but he escaped and made an alliance against King Henry with Henry's older brother Robert 'Curthose', Duke of Normandy. Soon thereafter, Henry found it politic to negotiate a peace with Robert which involved restoring Flambard to Durham. In 1104 Rannulf organised the re-interment of the relics of Cuthbert in the new Durham cathedral: the future king of Scots, Alexander I, brother of Queen Matilda (the Carham grantee) attended. (see Duncan 1975: 128).

# Carham:
# The castle of Wark-on-Tweed

## Norham Castle

The Normans built castles from the Tyne to the Tweed to control Northumberland (see Chapter 7). It is an indication of the peculiar position of the Prince-Bishops of the County Palatine of Durham in the 12th century that it was a bishop of Durham, Rannulf Flambard, who first built Norham Castle. Hugh de Puiset became bishop in 1153. In response to the Scots occupation of Northumberland (1136-1157), King Henry II of England (1154-1189) ordered the bishop to rebuild it much bigger and stronger. (www.english-heritage.org.uk)

In the nineteenth century, the ruined Norham Castle overlooking the Tweed was the subject of several paintings by J M W Turner.

## Wark-on-Tweed

Walter Espec's motte and bailey castle at Wark was built of timber. After being 'razed to the ground' by King David I of Scotland in 1138 it was rebuilt in stone. Being on the border, it was razed and rebuilt frequently over the ensuing centuries and it sometimes played host to visiting monarchs. The Northumberland County History (Vickers 1922: 46-71) records the following sequence:

1158 - the castle of Wark was fortified once again
1174 - King William [of Scotland] laid siege to Wark
1199 - 12 marks were expended in strengthening it
1216 - Wark was burnt to the ground
1255 - [Henry, king of England] now came in person to Wark
1292 - Edward I [of England] had paid his first visit to Wark
1296 - It was to Wark that Edward I proceeded [at] Easter
1310 - Edward II did manage to reach Wark
1318 - was compelled by famine to surrender to the Scots
1333 - recorded as 'ruined and broken.'
1390 - the castle lay in ruins

1399 - the Scots [-—] beat down the castle walls
1460 - the fortifications were dismantled [by the Scots]
1513 - Wark fell an easy prey to James IV [of Scotland]
1524 - the place was uninhabitable
1545 - adequately munitioned and in a proper state of defence
1547 - garrison raised to its usual complement of 200 men
1580 - so ruined that 'no man dare dwell [---]'

---

## A Fair Scottish Lady

The Roos family provide a romantic borders vignette.

'This Robert Roos [one of many in the family called Robert] was the last of his branch of the family to hold Wark, for in 1296, when war between Scotland and England was brewing, he was induced to throw in his lot with the former, seduced from his English allegiance by the charms of a fair Scottish lady [Christine Mowbray]. He tried to induce his uncle, William Roos, to join him, but the latter not only refused, but at once informed the English king of his kinsman's intention. As a result, a detachment, some thousand strong, was sent to prevent the surrender of Wark Castle to the enemy, but having camped at Presson for the night, it was surrounded and surprised by a Scottish force led by Robert Roos himself and very few escaped to tell the tale.' Vickers adds that Roos already had a wife, Laura. (Vickers 1922: 35)

---

## Roos of Wark

According to the Northumberland County History:

> The honour or barony [of Wark] was originally granted by Henry I to Walter Espec, lord of Helmsley, county York, who died in 1153, leaving as his heirs his three sisters, Hawise wife of William Bussey, Albreda wife of Nicholas Traille, and Adeline wife of Peter Roos. There seems reason to believe that, for a time at least, Henry II kept the inheritance in his own hands, but by 1191, Robert Roos, great grandson of Peter and Adeline, was in possession at Wark [-—] Robert's position was finally regularised in 1200, when King John confirmed him in all the honour which had belonged to Walter Espec ... (Vickers 1922: 31)

## Wark Castle - The Order of the Garter

The Order of the Garter was founded in the 1340s by Edward III of England with the motto 'Honi Soit Qui Mal Y Pense', which translates as 'Evil to him who thinks evil of it'. The order was probably formed to promote St George as patron saint of England and to strengthen Edward's claim to the throne of France; but why call it 'the Garter' and why give it this motto?

According to the website www.castlesfortsbattles.co.uk: (Accessed 11 May 2018)

> Wark Castle has been associated with the establishment of Edward III's Order of the Garter. After having defeated the 1342 siege, Edward and his court were present at Wark but during proceedings a garter worn by the Countess of Salisbury is said to have slipped from her leg. To prevent scurrilous comments against the wife of William Montagu [Earl of Salisbury] - his close friend and supporter - Edward fastened the Garter onto his own leg stating 'Evil to him who thinks evil of it'; Whether this story is true is hotly debated - and even if correct has also been linked with other locations including Calais.

Edward III was in the Tweed district at the time. In 1341 he spent 'Christmas at Melrose. During his stay he raided the forest of Ettrick 'in a very ill season'.' (Nicholson 1974: 143) The lady at the dance was Joan of Kent, described by Jean Froissart as 'the most beautiful woman in all the realm of England and the most loved' (Lawne 2016: 6). At the time she was married to William Montague, Earl of Salisbury. She later married Edward III's son, Edward 'the Black Prince'.

Polydore Virgil, the earliest source of the story, says that the garter incident happened in Calais after the battle of Crecy (1346). However, he was writing in the late sixteenth century, over 200 years later. Joan's most recent biographer, Penny Lawne, says that the garter incident probably never happened at all. (Lawne 2016: 86).

On the death of Elizabeth I of England in 1603, James VI of Scotland became James I of the United Kingdom of Great Britain and Ireland. Border wars between Scots and English became a thing of the past and, in 1633: 'what remained of the royal ordnance [at Wark] was removed to Berwick and London, and the castle was allowed once more to decay, [-—]' (Vickers p 72)

The Wark castle tower stood till at least 1863 but: 'the whole of the escarpment on which the north wall stood was then gradually crumbling, and a few years earlier this had compelled the removal of some of the masonry, as it had become dangerous to people crossing the ferry.' (Vickers p 72)

Photo 7: The Mound of Wark Castle in May 2018

.

# Bibliography

ADAMS, Max. 2014. *The King in the North* (London: Head of Zeus)

ADAMS, Max. 2017. *Alfred's Britain* (London: Head of Zeus)

ADOMNAN of Iona. 1995. *Life of St Columba*, Trans. Richard Sharpe (Middlesex, Penguin)

ANDERSON, Alan Orr. 1908. *Scottish Annals from English Chroniclers AD 500 to 1286* (London)

ANDERSON, Alan Orr. 1922. *Early Sources of Scottish History Vol. 1* (Edinburgh: Oliver & Boyd)

BARROW, G. W. S. 1973. *The Kingdom of the Scots* (New York: St Martin's Press)

BARROW, G. W. S. 1989. *Kingship and Unity: Scotland 1000-1306,* (Edinburgh: Edinburgh University Press)

BATES, Cadwallader. 1895. *History of Northumberland* (Morpeth, Reprint by Sandhill Press, 1996)

BEDE. 1968. *A History of the English Church and People,* Trans. by Leo Sherley-Price (Middlesex, Penguin)

BLAIR, Peter Hunter. 1963. 'Observations on the *Historia Regum* Attributed to Symeon of Durham', in Nora K Chadwick (Ed.). *Celt and Saxon: Studies in the Early British Border*, (Cambridge, Cambridge University Press): 63-118

BREEZE, David. 2006. *Roman Scotland: Frontier Country* (London: Batsford)

BROUN, Dauvit. 2005 'Alba: Pictish Homeland or Irish Offshoot?', in Pamela O'Neill (Ed). *Exile and Homecoming,* Papers from the 5th Australian Conference of Celtic Studies (Univ. of Sydney)

BROUN, Dauvit. 2013. *Scottish Independence and the Idea of Britain: From the Picts to Alexander III* (Edinburgh: Edinburgh University)

BROWN, P. Hume. 1902. *History of Scotland: Volume 1* (Cambridge: Cambridge University Press)

CARVER, Martin. 1998. *Sutton Hoo: Burial Ground of Kings?* (London: British Museum Press)

CHAMBERS, G. F. 1889. *Handbook of Descriptive and Practical Astronomy* (4th edn., Oxford)

CHAMBERS, James. 1981. T*he Norman Kings,* (London: Weidenfeld and Nicolson)

CLANCY, Thomas Owen. 1998. *The Triumph Tree: Scotland's earliest poetry AD 550-1350* (Edinburgh: Canongate)

CLARKSON, Tim. 2016. *Strathclyde and the Anglo-Saxons in the Viking Age* (Edinburgh: Birlinn)

COLGRAVE, Bertram (Trans.). 1939. *Two Lives of Saint Cuthbert:* University of Durham (Facsimile Edition, Christ the King Lib., USA)

DUNCAN, A. A. M. 1975. *Scotland: The Making of the Kingdom,* History of Scotland Vol 1 (Edin: Edinburgh Univ Press)

DUNCAN, A. A. M. 1976. The Battle of Carham, *Scottish Historical Review 55: 20-28*

DUNCAN, A. A. M. 2002. *The Kingship of the Scots 842-1292* (Edinburgh: Edin Univ Press)

FLETCHER, Richard. 2002. *Bloodfeud: Murder and Revenge in Anglo-Saxon England* (London, Allen Lane)

GALLYON, Margaret. 1977. *The Early Church in Northumbria* (Lavenham: Terence Dalton)

GILDAS. 1978. *The Ruin of Britain,* Trans. & Ed. by M. Winterbottom (Chichester: Phillimore)

HIGHAM, N. J. 1993. *The Kingdom of Northumbria AD 350-1100* (Stroud: Alan Sutton)

HOPE-TAYLOR, Brian. 1977. *Yeavering: An Anglo-British centre of early Northumbria,* (London: HMSO: DoE Arch. Reports No.7)

HOUSTON, R. A. and W. W. J. KNOX (Eds.). 2001. *The New Penguin History of Scotland from The Earliest Times to The Present Day* (London: Penguin)

HUMBLE, Richard. 1980. *The Saxon Kings* (London: Weidenfeld and Nicolson)

JACKSON, Anthony. 1984. *The Symbol Stones of Scotland* (Kirkwall: Orkney Press)

JOHNSON, Charles and H. A Cronne (Eds.). 1956. *Regesta Regum Anglo-Normannorum 1066-1154: Vol II Regesta Henrici Primi 1100-1135* (Oxford, Clarendon)

JONES, Gwyn. 1984. A *History of the Vikings (*Oxford: Univ. Press)

KAPELLE, William. 1979. *The Norman Conquest of the North* (London: Croom Helm)

KRONK, G. W. 1999. *Cometography: A Catalogue of Comets Vol. 1: Ancient to 1799* (Cambridge: Cambridge Univ Press) Vols. 1-6 (1999-2017)

LAPIDGE, Michael (Ed.).2008. *The Blackwell Encyclopedia of Anglo-Saxon England*

LAWNE, Penny. 2016. *Joan of Kent: The First Princess of Wales* (Stroud: Amberley)

LAYCOCK, Stuart. 2008. *Britannia: The Failed State (*Stroud: History Press)

LOMAS, Richard. 1996. *County of Conflict* (East Linton Scotland: Tuckwell)

Mac AIRT, S. and G. mac Niocaill (Eds. and Trans.). 1983. *Annals of Ulster* (Dublin)

McGUIGAN, Neil. 2015. *Neither Scotland nor England: Middle Britain, c.850–1150 (*Univ. of St Andrews: Unpub. PhD Thesis)

MACK, James L. 1926. *The Border Line* (Edinburgh: Oliver & Boyd)

MORRIS, Marc. 2008. A *Great and Terrible King: Edward I and the Forging of Britain* (London: Windmill)

NENNIUS. 1980. *British History and the Welsh Annals:* Trans. & Ed. by John Morris (Chichester: Phillimore)

NEVILLE, Cynthia. 1998. *Violence, Custom and Law* (Edinburgh: Edinburgh University Press)

NICHOLSON, Ranald. 1974. *Scotland: The Later Middle Ages:* The Edinburgh History of Scotland Vol.2 (Edinburgh: Edinburgh University Press)

ORAM, Richard. 2008. *David: The King Who Made Scotland* (Stroud: History Press)

OS-RB. 1978. *Roman Britain 4th Edition (*Southampton: Ordnance Survey)

PARFITT, Simon, et al. 2005. *The Earliest Record of Human Activity in Northern Europe (*http://ahobproject.org/: *The Ancient Human Occupation of Britain Project)*

PASSMORE, D.G. and Clive Waddington. 2009. *Managing Archaeological Landscapes in Northumberland: Till Tweed Studies Vols. 1 & 2,* (Oxford: Oxbow Books)

POOLE, Austin Lane. 1955. *Domesday Book to Magna Carta 1087-1216,* Oxford History of England Vol 3, (Oxford: Clarendon Press)

RAINE, Rev. James. 1852. T*he History and Antiquities of North Durham,* (Durham: Andrews)

ROACH, Levi. 2017. *Aethelred the Unready,* (London: Yale Univ)

ROLLASON, David. 2003. *Northumbria 500-1100: Creation and Destruction of a Kingdom,* (Cambridge: Cambridge University Press)

RONAY, Gabriel. 1989. *The Lost King of England: The East European Adventures of Edward the Exile,* (Woodbridge: Boydell)

SALWAY, Peter. 1981. *Roman Britain,* The Oxford History of England Vol 1A, (Oxford: Clarendon Press)

SCHROETER, J. Fr.1923. *Spezieller Kanon der zentralen Soone- und Mondfinsternisse* (Kristiania)

SIMEON of Durham. 1858. *A History of the Kings of England*, Joseph Stevenson (Trans.) (Facs. Reprint 1987: Lampeter, Wales: Llanerch)

SIMEON of Durham 1865. *A History of the Church of Durham*, Joseph Stevenson (Trans.) (Facs. Reprint 1993: Lampeter, Wales: Llanerch)

SIMEON of Durham.*1882. Symeonis Monachi Opera Omnia, Vol 1 and Vol 2,* Thomas Arnold (Ed) (London: Longman)

SIMPSON, Luisella. 1989. 'The King Alfred/St Cuthbert Episode in the *Historia de Sancto Cuthberto'*, in Bonner et al, *St Cuthbert: His Cult and Community to AD 1200,* (Woodbridge: Boydell)

SMITH, Ian. 1991. 'Sprouston Roxburghshire: an early Anglian centre of the eastern Tweed Basin' *Proc Soc. Antiq. Scot, 121: 261-294*

SOUTH, Ted Johnson, (Trans. & Ed.). 2002. *Historia de Sancto Cuthberto,* Anglo-Saxon Texts 3, (Cambridge: D S Brewer)

STENTON, Frank. 1971. *Anglo-Saxon England,* 3rd Edn. (Oxford: Oxford University Press)

SWANTON, Michael. 1996. *The Anglo-Saxon Chronicle* (New York: Routledge)

VICKERS, Kenneth. 1922. *A History of Northumberland Vol XI,* (London: Northumberland County History Committee)

WADDINGTON, Clive and David Passmore. 2004. *Ancient Northumberland,* (Wooler: Country Store)

WILKINSON, Frederick. 1973. *The Castles of England* (London: Letts)

WHITELOCK, Dorothy, (Trans. and Ed.). 1961. Anglo-*Saxon Chronicle* (Eyre & Spottiswoode, London)

WOOLF, Alex. 2007. *From Pictland to Alba 789-1070,* The New Edinburgh History of Scotland Vol 2, (Edinburgh: Edinburgh University Press)